C000279636

TAEKWONDO

TAEKWONDO

SPARRING STRATEGIES
FOR THE RING AND THE STREET

Adam Gibson

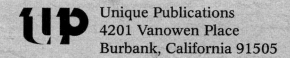

Unique Publications
4201 Vanowen Place
Burbank, California 91505

Disclaimer

Please note that the author and publisher of this book are NOT RESPONSIBLE in any manner whatsoever for any injury that may result from practicing the techniques and/or following the instructions given within. Since the physical activities described herein may be too strenuous in nature for some readers to engage in safely, it is essential that a physician be consulted prior to training.

First published in 2000 by Unique Publications

Copyright © 2000 by CFW Enterprises, Inc.

All rights reserved. No part of this publication may be reproduced or utilized in any form or by any means, electronic or mechanical, including photocopying, recording, or by any information storage and retrieval system, without prior written permission from Unique Publications.

Library of Congress Catalog Number: 00-135349

ISBN: 0-86568-186-4

Unique Publications
4201 Vanowen Place
Burbank, CA 91505
(800) 332–3330

First edition
05 04 03 02 01 00 99 98 97 1 3 5 7 9 10 8 6 4 2
Printed in the United States of America

CONTENTS

Introduction

This book presents taekwondo sparring training and strategies from a scientific perspective. Too many books waste pages repeating what others have done for well over a decade, doing nothing more than presenting history and tournament rules and illustrating basic kicking, punching, and patterns of the art. This may be great for the beginner, but not for the intermediate student, let alone the advanced practitioner. Moreover, to date, black belts and masters have had very few references from which to improve themselves and their fighting abilities.

Taekwondo Sparring Strategies for the Ring and the Street has changed all that. In this book you will find some of the most advanced master level concepts in existence, but so thoroughly explained and easy to understand that a white belt could absorb it. The book is broken down into sections that deal with specific aspects of sparring which most masters and instructors have failed to present in one complete book. In this book you will learn the most important and sought after information and concepts on physical and mental training for the martial arts. Advanced principles like: speed training, footwork, strength/flexibility training, endurance training, combination attacking methods, and defensive skills. We also present all the basic and advanced kicks, strikes, and blocks and give the reader tips of where they might use these techniques in a real combat situation. This book also contains chapters on recuperation and nutrition that will increase energy levels and help the athlete recover from workouts and injuries faster than normal. Also very few books teach the martial artist how to set up their opponent to enable you to create openings and score.

In short, this book was intended for beginners, black belts, top competitors, coaches, and masters of all different styles. So if you only buy one book on sparring, this one could last you a lifetime as a one-stop reference and wealth of knowledge.

PART ONE
PRELIMINARIES

Chapter 1
WARMING-UP

The purpose of warming-up is to ready the body for intense physical exercise and contact. Circulation is increased and adrenal glands are stimulated which in turn unlocks the body's advanced breathing and concentration capabilities while at the same time increasing one's ability to endure pain. Perhaps the most important feature of warming-up is that the body's susceptibility to minor and serious injury is greatly decreased.

The following are methods used for warming-up the body and should be part of your everyday training routine.

Cardio Warm-Ups

The recommended amounts of time on the following cardio warm-up exercises are not to build great amounts of endurance, but are recommended to prepare for a rigorous martial arts workout. Greater amounts of time should be spent on the exercises when you are doing a conditioning workout, as opposed to a technical workout. You will find more about endurance training later on in the chapter on endurance.

Since 20 minutes of cardio warm-up is sufficient for everyday workouts, pick any of the following and rotate them at will on different days to add variety to your training.

People with serious back problems should not engage in these exercises due to the impact involved. In any event, consult with your doctor before engaging in any physical activity.

Jumping Jacks

Starting with your hands at your sides and your feet together, jump up slightly and spread your legs apart as your hands come up and touch each other at the top (fig. 1). It is best to do a minimum of 50 jumping jacks per session, or for a specified period of time—say five minutes—using a stopwatch.

Light Running

This warm-up involves running in a circle and changing directions every 30 seconds or so at various speeds for a period of five to 10 minutes per workout (fig. 2).

Please note that running on a padded floor or grass field is a lot easier on the joints, leading to less chances of injury.

Running on the Spot

While standing up straight alternate lifting your knees up and down and alternate lifting your arms up and down as if you were running but not going anywhere. It is best to do around 50 knee lifts or more per workout, which equals to about two minutes in time per workout (fig. 3).

If you are already fit and wish to increase the difficulty of this exercise, raise your knees higher (waist-level and above).

Jumping Rope

There are many variations for jumping rope. You can jump over the rope one foot at a time (alternating) or you can hop on one foot a few times and then switch feet every few jumps. You can also jump over the rope both feet at a time (fig. 4). It is best to do 200 or more rope jumps per workout, which can be broken up into three rounds of three minutes each.

Bicycle or Stationary Bike

Find a nice trail or flat road to go bicycling on or ride on a stationary bike varying the resistance controls. Five to fifteen minutes per workout should be sufficient.

Stair Machine

While standing up straight hold onto the handles and push up and down, utilizing the resistance controls to make the exercise more intense. Five to 15 minutes of stair machine is a good place to start (fig. 5).

This exercise is ideal for people who have back and joint problems because joint stress is greatly reduced due to the lack of bouncing and impact shock.

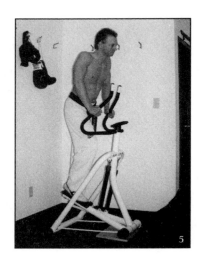

Warming Up the Joints

Always practice the following exercises slowly in order to properly warm-up each respective area and avoiding injury.

Side-to-Side Neck Turns

Standing-up straight with your hands on your hips, lean your head to the left (stretching the right-side of your neck), and then to the right (stretching the left-side of your neck) (figs. 6–8). Five to 10 neck turns per side should be sufficient to loosen up the area.

Do not do this exercise fast as it can injure your neck. Always perform slow and smooth movements.

Up-and-Down Neck Movements

While standing up straight with your hands on your hips, bend your neck forward (stretching the back of your neck) and then lean your head slightly backwards (stretching the front of your neck) (figs. 9, 10). Five to 10 neck turns per side should be sufficient to loosen up the area.

Do not do this exercise fast as it can injure your neck. Always perform slow and smooth movements.

Three-Point Neck Pivot

Standing up straight. Hold your arms out at shoulder level (with your thumbs pointing toward the ceiling), turn your head and look at your right thumb, then turn your head facing directly in front of you, and then turn your head and look at your left thumb (figs. 11–13). Turning your head five to 10 times to

each direction should be sufficient.

Always start this exercise slow and gradually increase the speed carefully. Never go fast if you have spinal injuries or muscular problems in your neck and/or back.

Neck Rotations

Standing up straight with your hands on your hips. Rotate your neck counter-clockwise one full revolution, keeping your eyes open at all times (figs. 14–17). First rotate your head five to 10 times in the clockwise direction and then five to 10 times counter-clockwise.

Do not do this exercise fast as it can injure your neck. Always practice slow and smooth movements.

Shoulder Circles

Standing up straight. Rotate your arm very slowly backwards in a circular fashion as high as possible and then down as low as possible completing a full circle. Perform five to 10 forward rotations before continuing in the opposite direction another five to 10 rotations (figs. 18–21).

Do not flail your arms at high speeds. Always execute each rotation slowly with full control over the muscles in your arm.

Side-to-Side Waist Bends

Stand straight up with your
hands on your hips and lean to
your right side and then lean to
your left side. Between five and
10 bends to each side should
be sufficient (figs. 22–24).

Forward and Backward Waist bends

Start standing up straight with your hands on your hips and with your eyes looking straight ahead. Bend forward with your back parallel to the floor, stretching the back of your buttocks and legs. From here, stand up straight and then lean backwards, stretching your abdominals. Between five and 10 forward and backward bend sets per workout should be sufficient to loosen the area (figs. 25–28).

Waist Rotations

Stand straight with your hands on your hips and rotate your upper body clockwise, making a full circle five to 10 rotations per direction (figs. 29–33).

Knee Circles

With your knees slightly bent and your hands placed just above your knee-caps (with your feet no more than six-inches apart) gently rotate your knees in small circles, five to 10 times in each direction (figs. 34–36).

Ankles

While standing up straight place your body weight on your right foot while touching the ball of your left foot on the ground and rotating it clockwise and counter-clockwise very gently, five to 10 times in each direction (fig. 37).

This exercise is highly recommended for people who have old and current ankle injuries.

Wrists

Rotate your wrists clockwise and counter-clockwise, five to 10 times per direction.

Side Leg-Swing

Place both hands on a chair or support about waist-level while pointing your heels and buttocks away from the chair. Look over your left shoulder and swing your left leg up as high as possible without any discomfort in a sidekick position (meaning your foot should be held sideways) (figs. 38, 39). Then switch and repeat on the other side. Do a set of 10 side leg swings per side.

Front Leg-Swing

With your right hand on a chair or support about waist high and your toes pointing perpendicular (to the chair) swing your left leg up to your chest or shoulder (or as high as possible without discomfort) in a front kick position keeping the leg straight (figs. 40, 41). Then switch and repeat on the other side. Do a set of 10 front leg swings per side.

Chapter 2
STRETCHING

Flexibility is the mobility of the joints and the elasticity of the muscle fibers, tendons, and ligaments. Flexibility has an influence over all aspects of fighting. Power is greatly hindered without full range of motion and speed is decreased when muscles are too tight. Endurance levels are decreased without flexibility training because extra effort is required for basic and advanced movements. Kicking high to the head with power and accuracy is next to impossible without proper flexibility.

Morning Stretches

Morning stretches are exercises that provide full range of motion in the joint areas without having a full-workout to accomplish this. Such exercises include: arm-circles, neck-circles, torso-twists, and various leg-swings.

Great benefits can be acquired from doing these stretches every morning. When you first awake in the morning your body is stiff from sleeping, that is to say inactivity. In order to loosen up the body without hurting oneself these are the safest form of exercise that your body will respond to first thing in the morning.

Another benefit is that if confronted in an altercation in the street (a situation where you will not have time to stretch) you will already be loose enough to execute punches and kicks (high and low) with minimal risk of tearing joint and muscle tissues.

A third benefit is that continual practice of morning stretches promotes total body stress relief (relaxation of the muscle tissues) and increased circulation that in turn will aid in recovering from mild-to-intense work-outs.

Recommended Daily Routine

It is recommended that you perform these stretches seven days a week, waiting at least 10 to 15 minutes after waking-up to give your body time to adjust. So in those minutes prior have a glass of juice, brush your teeth, shave, wash your face, etc. You may wish to perform these exercises before going into the shower because you may sweat a little while doing them. And they should only take you a maximum of five minutes to perform. Remember it is not a race when stretching, so do not flail your arms, legs, and neck at high speeds, as this can only lead to injury. Only use controlled medium-paced movements.

Morning stretches should also be done as a part of your regular workout, as the first phase of stretching, right after your cardio warm-up. Do 10 to 12 repetitions per side for all stretches.

Muscular Stretching

The purpose of muscular stretching is to loosen the muscles, ligaments, and tendons through holding a given position for approximately 20 seconds. This type of stretching helps prepare the muscles and other tissues for the abuse they will take during striking, kicking, throwing, and other strenuous activities that martial art training entails. Never try to push yourself to your maximum during muscular stretching because this tires out the muscles, which in turn will give you an inferior workout.

Practicing the splits is generally not recommended prior to your kicking workout, specifically because it can be one of the most energy depleting stretches unless you're one of these people who can drop into splits cold with little effort.

Remember, there are always exceptions to the rules of conditioning, but generally the above works pretty well for most martial arts practitioners.

Developmental Stretching

Developmental stretches are exercises that actually lengthen muscles, ligaments, and tendons to provide higher levels of flexibility. Developmental stretches are exercises such as front and side-splits held for 30 seconds or more. Muscular stretching can also be considered as developmental stretching provided the positions are held for 30 seconds or more.

The following are exercises designed to sustain and develop high levels of flexibility needed for combat.

Stretch 1

Place your feet about two shoulder widths apart with your hands flat on the floor. Shift your body to the right and then shift your body to the left. Reach with both hands to touch your right foot and then reach with both hands to touch your left foot (figs. 1–5). Repeat.

Stretch 2

With your fists at your sides, your front knee bent, your back leg straight, and head up, sink into a walking stance position with your toes pointing straight ahead and with your shoulders square. Switch legs and then repeat this position on the other side. Perform this stretch one to two times per side at a count of 10–20 seconds per stretch (figs. 6, 7).

If you keep your feet flat on the ground, this will stretch the front of the thigh and the back of the calf. Moreover, the lower you sink, bending your front knee, the more intense the stretch becomes.

Stretch 3

Spread your legs apart, grab your ankles, and pull your head to the floor and hold. This stretches the inner portions and back of your thighs. Do this as a warm-up stretch for a

count of 20 seconds, and as a cool-down stretch for a count of 30 or more seconds. For a deeper stretch, point your toes toward the ceiling and then bend forward (fig. 8).

Stretch 4

Spread your legs apart as above, but stretch each leg individually. First stretch down to the left foot, grabbing your toes and the side of your foot and touching your head to

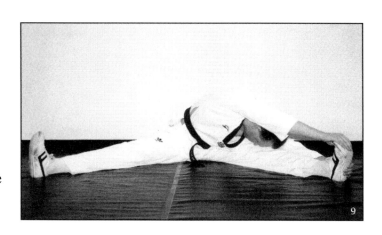

your knee and hold. Repeat on the right side. Do this as a warm-up stretch for a count of 20 seconds, and as a cool-down stretch for a count of 30 or more seconds (figs. 9, 10).

Stretch 5

Tuck your right foot in with your left leg out straight and grab the side of your foot with one hand and your toes with the other. Try to touch your head to your knee (but only bend to the point of tension—not pain) and hold. Repeat on the right side. Do this as a warm-up stretch for a count of 20 seconds, and as a cool-down stretch for a count of 30 or more seconds (figs. 11, 12).

This exercise stretches the calf and the back of the thigh, and if you pull your heel up off the ground it will intensify the stretch.

Stretch 6

With your feet extended in front of you try to reach for your ankles or toes and pull your head down to the point of tension. This will stretch the back of your calves, thighs, buttocks, and lower-back. Do this as a warm-up stretch for a count of 20 seconds, and as a cool-down stretch for a count of 30 or more seconds (fig. 13).

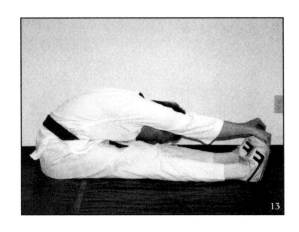

Stretch 7

With your legs about two shoulder widths apart, bend forward, grab both ankles, and pull your head in between your legs and hold. Do this as a warm-up stretch for a count of 20 seconds, and as a cool-down stretch for a count of 30 or more seconds. And be sure to keep your legs straight, body relaxed, and don't lose your balance (fig. 14).

This exercise stretches the backs of the calves and thighs, buttocks, and upper-back. It is also easier on the lower back than the above stretch.

Stretch 8

While sitting on the floor, pull your heels in towards your groin, push your knees down to the floor or to the point of tension, stretching the inner portions of your thighs. Do this as a warm-up stretch for a count of 20 seconds, and as a cool-down stretch for a count of 30 or more seconds (figs. 15, 16).

I do not recommend the second variation of this exercise, for if you do not have the flexibility right off the bat you can get seriously injured. But, if you must use a partner, I would suggest only having your partner stand behind you and gently push their body weight down using your hands.

Stretch 9

Place your foot on a chair or support and straighten-out your knee (be careful not to hyper-extend your knee). This stretches the back of your calf and thigh. Do this as a warm-up stretch for a count of 20 seconds, and as a cool-down stretch for a count of 30 or more seconds (fig. 17).

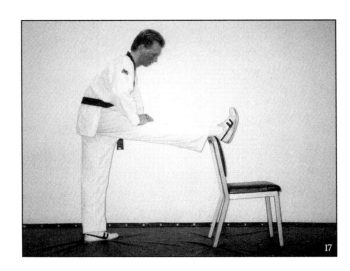

Be sure to keep your toes pointing up toward the ceiling and don't lose your balance. If you have poor balance find something stable to hold on to.

Stretch 10

With your feet about two shoulder widths apart clasp your hands together and let your shoulders roll forward. This will stretch the upper-back and the backs of your calves and thighs. Do this as a warm-up stretch for a count of 20 seconds, and as a cool-down stretch for a count of 30 or more seconds (figs. 18, 19).

As this stretch is usually used to stretch the upper-back and other stretches should be used to stretch the calves and the upper thighs. In other words, don't rely on just one stretch to cover many body parts because some stretches don't do as good a job as others or they may hit the muscle from a different angle, causing some different effects.

Stretch 11

The front split is performed by placing one foot in front of your upper-body (with the toes pointing up towards the ceiling) and the other foot behind (positioned either sideways or on the instep of the foot) while keeping the upper body up straight and shoulders as square as possible. This exercise stretches the top of the inner thigh, hip flexor, and the back of the thigh (fig. 20).

As an advanced variation, repeat the above except bend forward at the hips and try to touch your head to your knee (fig. 21).

Do this as a cool-down stretch for 30 or more seconds. It should also be done at the end of your workout only because it can rob your muscles of energy needed for a strenuous work-out load.

Stretch 12

You can either stand or lay down for this exercise while your partner gently pushes your leg toward you. Go only to the point of tension and concentrate on relaxing your muscles. If you choose the standing variation make sure you hold hands with your partner for balance and safety purposes. This exercise stretches the same muscles as the above stretch (fig. 22).

Do this as a cool-down stretch for 30 or more seconds. And never force your partner past their point of tension. Always wait until they are relaxed before you attempt to get more of a stretch.

Stretch 13

From the standing position place your foot sideways on a partner's shoulder with your toes pointing down. The partner begins from a squatting position and then stands up slowly until you reach your point of tension. This exercise focuses mostly on stretching the inner portion of the upper-thigh (fig. 23).

Do this as a cool-down stretch for 30 or more seconds. Make sure your hips are properly aligned for this stretch by pointing the toes of the supporting leg away from your partner while simultaneously having your buttocks facing them.

Stretch 14

With your legs about two shoulder widths apart sink into a low squatting position using your elbows for support. Make sure you keep your spine as straight as possible with your eyes looking straight ahead. This will stretch the inner portions of the thighs (fig. 24).

Stretch 15

While lying flat on your back with your buttocks and legs against a wall allow gravity to spread them apart until they cannot separate any further. This will stretch the inner portions of the thighs (fig. 25).

Stretch 16

With your legs spread apart while facing the wall try to spread them apart further by pushing yourself against the wall trying to place your whole upper body flat against it. Concentrate on relaxing all your muscles until they are loose and then try to get closer to the wall again (fig. 26).

Stretch 17

Using a partner, spread your legs apart and get them to place the bottoms of their feet against the inner portions of your ankles and hold on to your belt or wrists. From there get them to gently push your legs out further only going to your point of tension. Concentrate on relaxing until your legs feel a little looser and get your partner to gently stretch them out further (fig. 27).

The person who is being stretched should always be the one who is in control of the intensity of the stretch. Never let your partner judge for you. He cannot feel whether or not he's stretching you or just plain hurting you.

Stretch 18

With your legs crossed, bend over and touch the floor in front of you and then gently cross your legs keeping your back straight. Make sure you cross your legs the other way as well to get an equal stretch for both legs (fig. 28).

Do this as a warm-up stretch for a count of 20 seconds, and as a cool-down stretch for a count of 30 or more seconds to stretch your calves, backs of the thighs, buttocks, and lower-back.

Stretch 19

Sit on the floor and place your right foot on the outer side of your left knee and turn your upper body clockwise until you can see the wall behind you. Support yourself with your right hand. Repeat on the opposite side (figs. 29, 30).

Do this as a warm-up stretch for a count of 20 seconds, and as a cool-down stretch for a count of 30 or more seconds to stretch the hips, buttocks, and obliques.

Stretch 20

While lying on the
ground bend your
right knee and place
the outer portion of
your left ankle on
your right knee and
pull your right knee
in toward your chest
until you reach the
point of tension and
hold. Do this as a
warm-up stretch for
a count of 20 seconds,
and as a cool-down
stretch for a count of
30 or more seconds
to stretch the buttocks
(figs. 31, 32).

Stretch 21

While sitting on the floor grab your foot, pull it into your chest (cradling it like a baby), and twist your upper body to gently work the hip joint. Do this as a warm-up stretch for a count of 20 seconds, and as a cool-down stretch for a count of 30 or more seconds to stretch the buttocks and hips (fig. 33).

Stretch 22

While standing on one foot grab your knee with both hands and pull it in toward your chest. Make sure you keep your back and neck straight. Do this for 10 to 20 seconds per leg to stretch the buttocks and hips (fig. 34).

Stretch 23

While standing on one foot grab the ball of the opposite foot and extend your leg out straight, placing one arm out for balance. Do this for 10 to 20 seconds per leg to stretch the calves, backs of the thighs, and the buttocks (fig. 35).

Stretch 24

Place one foot in front of your body and one leg behind. Keep your front knee bent on a 90 to 120-degree angle with your shoulders square. Also keep your shin and instep parallel to the floor. To intensify the stretch shift forward toward your front knee (fig. 36).

Warm-up 20 seconds per side per workout, and cool-down 30 or more seconds per side per workout to stretch the hip-flexor and the front of the thigh.

Stretch 25

Place one foot in front and the other behind you. Bend your rear leg and straighten-out your front leg, pull your head down to your knee, and hold. Do this for 10 to 20 seconds to stretch the calves, backs of the legs, and buttocks (fig. 37).

Stretch 26

While keeping your legs straight walk across the floor pulling your legs up to your hands. Do this for 30 to 60 seconds per workout to stretch the backs of the thighs, calves, and buttocks (fig. 38).

Stretch 27

From the standing position cross your arms in front of you, then swing them to touch them behind you. Do 10 per workout to stretch the chest and the back (figs. 39, 40).

Stretch 28

From a standing position with your elbows at shoulder height, rotate the hips clockwise to see the wall behind you. Repeat in the other direction. This stretches the obliques, abdominals, and lower back (figs. 41–43).

Stretch 29

While lying with your back flat on the floor, place your legs sideways with your knees pointing to your left and place your arms pointing to your right. Make sure you concentrate on relaxing as much as possible to properly loosen the spine and obliques. Hold for a count of 15 to 20 seconds per side per workout to stretch the spine and stretch the obliques (figs. 44, 45).

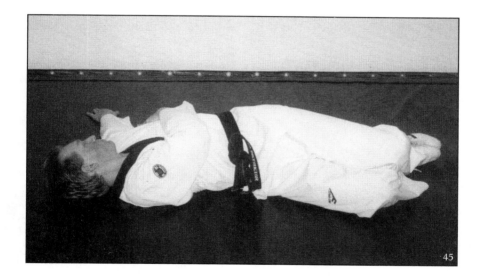

Stretch 30

To perform the bridging exercise start by lying on the floor and place your hands above your head with the palm heels pointing the opposite direction of your body. Bend your knees, placing your feet flat on the floor. Slowly inch your feet up forming the shape of a bridge. Do this as a cool down for 20 to 30 seconds to stretch the abdominals and chest (fig. 46).

Stretch 31

While lying with your stomach on the floor, place your hands flat on the floor beside you like in a push-up position. Then push your upper body up off

of the floor while keeping your legs on the floor. Only push up until you can feel the point of tension. Use this stretch after any abdominal routine for 20 to 30 seconds to loosen up your midsection (fig. 47).

Stretch 32

Clasp your hands behind your back and pull until you reach the point of tension. Hold for a count of 15 to 20 seconds to stretch the triceps (fig. 48).

Stretch 33

Utilizing a partner, get them to grab your wrists (placing them parallel to the floor) and gently pull them together until you reach the point of tension or your hands touch one another. Hold for a count of 15 to 20 seconds to stretch the inner portions of the shoulders and the chest (fig. 49).

Stretch 34

Place your left arm behind your back with the elbow pointing upward and gently push downward with your right hand until you reach the point of tension. Hold for a count of 15 to 20 seconds to stretch the shoulder (fig. 50).

Stretch 35

Grab your right hand with your left and bend your wrist to the point of tension with the palm of your right hand facing your biceps. Hold for a count of five to 10 seconds to stretch the wrist (fig. 51).

Stretch 36

From a relaxed fighting stance lift your right knee and pivot your hips to your left and draw an imaginary circle with your knee and finish your circle with your knee pointing to your right. Do 10 repetitions to stretch the hip joint and the muscles surrounding it (figs. 52–55).

This is a good replacement exercise for the next stretch if you are currently having back problems, as less stress is placed on the lower back if the knee is kept bent.

Stretch 37

From a relaxed fighting stance, keep your right knee straight and swing your leg in a circular motion, drawing a big circle and return to the starting position. Make sure your leg swing, at it's peak, is no lower than chest-level. As you progress you should be able to get your foot well above head-level. Do 10 circles per leg to stretch the hips and the surrounding muscles (figs. 56–59).

56

57

58

59

Stretch 38

From a relaxed fighting
stance, keeping your knee
bent, swing it up toward
your chest. Do 10 per leg
to stretch the hips and
the surrounding muscles
(figs. 60, 61).

This is an easier version
of the next stretch and is
ideal for someone who
is currently experiencing
lower-back problems.

Stretch 39

From a relaxed fighting stance, while keeping your knee straight, swing your leg straight up, about head-level or higher, and try to touch your thigh to your chest. Do 10 per leg to stretch the hip joint and the muscles surrounding it (figs. 62, 63).

Chapter 3
CONDITIONING

Physical endurance is the ability to exert muscular force repetitively over an extended period of time. Endurance is probably the greatest physical factor in all of fighting that can decide the outcome of a fight. When your endurance is greater than your opponent's you can give and receive punishment for longer periods of time—giving you one of the greatest edges possible. If skills are equal and you can out-last your opponent, you will win!

Mental endurance is also a part of combat and training, for without it you could not push yourself to your physical limits and potential during an intense or difficult situation.

The following exercises are designed to develop in you high levels of physical and mental endurance.

Aerobic Exercises

Jumping Jacks/Rope Skipping

Fifteen to 30 minutes of jumping jacks and skipping rope, three to six times a week will help to develop high levels of physical and mental endurance and mind-muscle coordination necessary for combat.

Sprinting

Sprinting is essential to developing your wind. After a proper warm-up it is good to spend five to 10 minutes executing sprinting drills on days you are working on conditioning only. Avoid doing heavy sprinting drills on days that you are working on kicking as sprinting takes a lot of energy out of your legs, which you will need to practice properly.

Bag Work

Punching and kicking the bag is no doubt one of the best ways a fighter can develop their endurance while also improving their striking skills. Striking a punching bag is a little different than hitting hand-held targets because the latter allow you to follow through with your technique—as when practicing in the air. A punching bag creates much more resistance depending on the weight, what's in it, and if someone is holding it. Therefore, this exercise is for the serious practitioner, especially those involved in full-contact. Also you will learn quickly how to properly hit without injuring yourself while at the same time developing power in your techniques. Those of you training for full-contact should do 30 to 60 minutes of bag work two to three times a week.

Circuit Training

Circuit training is endurance training interspersed with strength training. An example of this would be if you did jumping-jacks followed by 30 reps of dumb-bell curls.

Sparring

Sparring is essential to learning how to apply taekwondo in the ring and on the street. Thirty to 60 minutes of sparring, dispersed over two to three minute rounds, done three to five times a week, will dramatically increase your endurance as well as your combat skills. This is probably the best exercise for developing endurance for combat because sparring is the closest thing to real combat.

Interval Training

Interval-training is low intensity endurance training interspersed with high intensity endurance training. An example of this would be if you went out for a 30 minute run and every four or five minutes you sprinted for 20 to 30 seconds as fast as you could, immediately after returning to regular running speed.

Target Drills

Target drills are an excellent method for building endurance because there are so many different exercise variations that can be utilized to avoid boredom. One or two targets can be used at a time. Target drills can be used for endurance training while at the same time improving your footwork, speed, power, timing, precision, and offensive/defensive strategies. The only disadvantage to target drills is that if you don't have a partner to hold them and you only have them mounted on the wall, you become more limited in the complexity of your drills.

Endurance Exercises

Single Low Kick

While low kicking will enhance your endurance whether you practice on a target or in the air, it will bring you minimal results. For best results, try doing between five and 100 kicks, per kick, per leg, per session at low intensity (fig. 1).

Single High Kick

High kicking will increase your endurance much more than low kicking simply because you have to lift that heavy leg much higher to reach the target. Therefore, more work is being done. For best results, try doing between five and 100 kicks, per leg, per session at medium intensity (fig. 2).

Continuous Kick

Kicking a target varying the height of the kick each time continuously without stopping for 10 or more kicks is extremely beneficial for developing endurance. For best results, try doing between 10 and 30 kicks, per leg, per session at high intensity. Remember, the faster your body moves the more intense the drill becomes. This applies to basically all endurance type exercises (figs. 3, 4).

Bag Work

Kicking and punching the heavy bag in rounds can be one of the most intense of all endurance exercises because of the resistance training it offers. When training for competition always practice while wearing a mouth guard so you can develop a proper breathing

pattern. For best results, try doing between three and 16 rounds of one to three minutes per round. For maximum benefits always make your training harder than the event you are preparing for (figs. 5, 6).

Moving Target Training

A moving target-drill is when the target holder moves around the training area placing the target randomly by heightening it, lowering it, moving backwards and forwards, and moving in circles. The goal of the kicker or puncher is to react to the target holder offensively and defensively. For best results, try doing between two to five rounds per side of one to three minutes in duration each (fig. 7).

Sprinting

Sprinting is one of the most universal training drills for fighting because it benefits so many areas, such as: speed, explosive power, strength, and endurance. I have chosen to put it in the endurance section because regular paced running helps for overall endurance, or the slower paced sections of

a fight, and sprinting helps during the more intense periods. An example could be a combination of three or more kicks done as fast as you can. Another example is during heavy exchanges where there is constant kicking and punching (fig. 8).

For best results try to run distances of 20 to 100 meters five to 10 times. This is not a good exercise for athletes who have ankle, knee, or back problems.

Here I am pictured with one of my best friends, Robert Esmie—World Relay Champion and Olympic Gold Medalist in Atlanta, 1996. He is one of the fastest men alive and is believed by many to have the fastest explosive start in the world. If there's anyone who knows anything about the science of sprinting it's gonna be this guy.

Part Two

BASICS

Chapter 4
STANCES AND FOOTWORK

Fighting Stances

The stance that one uses while in combat usually reflects his personality, martial art background, and overall knowledge of fighting. Whether you fight in a boxer-style stance or in a side-stance there are some key principles that all fighters should understand no matter what style they practice. The following are some pictures to illustrate those principles.

A Wide Stance

Never spar with your stance more than two shoulder widths apart because you cannot move quickly. That is, footwork cannot be executed correctly without extra effort (wasting time) and your kicking

and punching skills will lack power and effectiveness (fig. 1).

A Medium Stance

A medium stance is very effective because your feet are wide enough apart for good stability and close enough together so that you can execute footwork quickly (fig. 2).

Straight Knee Stance

Never keep your knees straight while sparring/fighting because you will not react properly. Footwork is greatly hampered (slowed-down) as in order to move you must bend your knees and push in the direction you wish to go. By keeping

your knees bent like coiled springs you will be ready to pounce like a cat. If you keep them straight you will move like a pregnant penguin (fig. 3).

Knees Slightly Bent Stance

If your knees are always slightly bent you will always be ready to attack, sidestep, or counter. Notice that the more you bend your knees the faster and the more powerful your footwork will become. But do not over bend your knees (like in low squat) because this leads to knee damage, especially in growing teenagers (fig. 4).

Defensive Footwork

Retreat Step

From a solid fighting stance, gently step back about six to 10 inches with your rear foot, then slide your front foot back the same amount of space, returning to a solid fighting stance.

Quick Retreat Step

This is a linear maneuver whose main purpose is to quickly evade a deep attack. From a solid fighting stance, quickly bring your front foot to your rear foot then step backward with your rear foot, returning to a solid fighting stance (figs. 5–7).

Stance Switch

This is a pivoting
footwork maneuver
whose main purpose
is to evade medium to
fairly deep attacks while
changing leads. From a
solid fighting stance, step
backward, switch sides
(change leads), and return
to a solid fighting stance
(figs. 8–10).

Right Angle Cut

This is a straight line/lateral footwork maneuver whose main purpose is to evade the opponent by moving off the line of attack. With this footwork, there are any number of kicks you can execute, such as hook kick, sidekick, turn back kick, or spinning hook kick.

From a solid fighting stance, pull your front foot to your rear foot, then step your front foot toward your open side and trail your rear foot in behind your front foot (figs. 11–14).

Front view, 11

Front view, 12

Front view, 13

Front view, 14

Blindside Cut

This is a lateral/pivot footwork maneuver whose main purpose is to evade the opponent's attack by side-stepping toward your blindside to move off the line of attack.

From a solid fighting stance, step backward toward your blindside on a 45-degree angle with your front foot and pivot on your front foot about 90-degrees (figs. 15–18).

Sidestep (Open Side)

This is a lateral footwork maneuver whose main purpose is to evade your opponent by side-stepping to your open side.

From a solid fighting stance, step toward your open-side with your rear foot, trail your front foot behind, and return to a balanced fighting stance (figs. 19–21).

Side Step (Blind Side)

This is a lateral footwork maneuver whose main purpose is to evade your opponent's attack by side stepping to your blind-side off the line of fire.

From a solid fighting stance, step toward your blindside with your front foot, trail your rear foot with you, and return to a solid fighting stance (figs. 22–24).

Pivot (Blind Side)

This is a pivot maneuver
whose main purpose is
to evade an attack by
pivoting off the line
of fire.

From a solid fighting
stance, pivot 90-degrees
on your front foot toward
your blind side (figs.
25, 26).

Stance Switch

This is a pivot footwork maneuver whose main purpose is to confuse the opponent before you attack by quickly switching sides.

From a solid fighting stance, switch sides in mid-air, not moving forward or backwards. Do a complete 180-degree pivot (figs. 27–29).

Offensive Footwork

Short Step

This is a linear footwork maneuver whose main purpose is to move you a few inches closer to your opponent.

From a solid fighting stance, take a small step forward with your front foot, trail your rear foot toward your front foot, ending in a balanced fighting stance (figs. 30–32).

Push Step

This is a linear footwork maneuver whose main purpose is to fake an opponent and/or to cover short to medium amounts of distance between you and your opponent.

From a solid fighting stance, push hard off your rear foot, step forward with your front foot, trail your rear foot up toward your front foot, and end in a balanced fighting stance (figs. 33–35).

Quick Advance

This is a linear footwork maneuver whose main purpose is to quickly cover large distances between you and your opponent.

From a solid fighting stance, slide your rear foot up to your front foot while keeping your head level, step forward with your front foot, ending in a solid fighting stance (figs. 36–38).

Step-Through

This is a pivot footwork maneuver whose main purpose is to cover large distances between you and your opponent.

From a solid fighting stance, step forward with your rear foot and, while protecting your centerline, pivot 180-degrees, ending in a solid fighting stance (figs. 39–41).

Reverse Step-Through

This is a pivot footwork maneuver whose main purpose is to cover far distances between you and your opponent.

From a solid fighting stance, pivot on your front foot to turn your back to your opponent, then switch sides (change leads), and end in a balanced fighting stance (figs. 42–45).

Hop Step

This is a linear footwork maneuver whose main purpose is to cover a short distance between you and your opponent to set up a kick, such as a lead leg roundhouse kick, sidekick, and hook kick. From a solid fighting stance, lean back onto your rear foot while chambering your lead leg for a kick, push off your rear foot and simultaneously hop forward (covering distance), execute a kick, and return to a solid fighting stance (figs. 46–50).

Cross Behind

This is a linear footwork maneuver whose main purpose is to cover far distances quickly, and is excellent for countering attacks using a lead punch or backfist.

From a solid fighting stance, cross your rear foot behind your front foot and then step forward with your lead foot to return to a balanced fighting stance (figs. 51–53).

Cross In Front

This is a linear footwork maneuver whose main purpose is to
quickly cover medium to far
distances between you and
your opponent. This footwork
is usually incorporated with
a lead leg roundhouse kick.

From a solid fighting stance,
cross your rear foot in front of
your lead foot (remaining sideways) then step forward with your
lead foot, ending in a balanced fighting stance (figs. 54–56).

Chapter 5
BLOCKS

High Block

From a fighting stance, raise your lead arm above your head and block with your forearm. Your forearm must be held on a 45-degree angle, with your fist higher than your elbow. If it is parallel to the ground the power of the attacking blow will be focused on your elbow, making it much easier for the attacker to smash down your block (figs. 1, 2).

Inside Middle Block

From a side fighting stance, sweep your lead hand in front of your stomach in an upward, semi-circular motion (clockwise), deflecting the attack to the outside of your body with your forearm (figs. 3–5).

Outside Middle Block

From a forward stance, sweep your lead arm horizontally across, deflecting the attack with the forearm (figs. 6–8).

Low Block

From a side or forward
stance (with both guards up),
extend your lead arm down
in a semi-circular motion,
brushing or deflecting the
attack to the outside of your
body with your closed or
open forearm or hand
(figs. 9–11).

Double X Block (low)

From a forward stance
(with both guards up),
cross your forearms in
front of your body, push
downward on a 45-degree
angle to jam the oppo-
nent's attack with your
forearms. If your left leg
is forward your left forearm should be under your
right arm, and vice-versa
(figs. 12, 13).

Double X Block (high)

From a forward stance (with both guards up), cross your forearms in front of your body, push upward on a 45-degree angle to jam the opponent's downward attack with your forearms. If your left leg is forward your left forearm should be under your right arm, and vice-versa (figs. 14, 15).

Chapter 6
PUNCHES AND STRIKES

The Jab

The jab is an extremely useful tool in both offensive and defensive situations, although it is typically used to set-up other punches or kicks while on the offensive. In a martial arts sparring or even a self-defense situation you could use a jab to fake high to the opponent's head, enticing them to draw their guards up high, while you quickly sneak in a low sidekick to a lower area, like the knee or mid-section.

From a solid fighting stance, push off your rear foot and extend your lead elbow. Tighten up your arm only on impact (figs. 1, 2).

Vertical Punch

Vertical punches can be performed with great power using both the front and rear hands. Moreover, the alignment of the fist, wrist, and forearm is more stable than the traditional horizontal punch. The vertical punch is most commonly seen in Chinese style martial arts, but can be easily integrated into any martial artist's hand technique repertoire. To increase this punch's power and develop good forearm stabilization you must practice knuckle push-ups in the vertical punch position on a daily basis.

From a solid fighting stance, push off your rear-foot and step forward with your front-foot, while extending your lead-arm, striking the target with your fist vertically up and down (figs. 3, 4).

Reverse Punch

The reverse punch is one of the most commonly used punches in competition and street self-defense. When utilizing this punch on the offensive it is usually wise to set it up with another technique because the rear hand can be fairly telegraphic. When using it on the defensive the reverse punch usually works best after some sort of block.

From a solid fighting stance, push off your rear-foot, and extend your rear-elbow while turning your upper-body, tighten up your arm only on impact (figs. 5, 6).

Backfist

The backfist is an excellent technique for point competition and street self-defense because of its blinding speed. The backfist is an excellent opening technique for combination attacks because it is generally thrown from the lead hand like the jab. Most people don't realize that the backfist and the jab are fairly different from one another and have their own unique purposes.

The backfist is like the roundhouse kick because it can be thrown from various angles, allowing one to find many options in scoring. The key to developing speed in this technique is to try to snap the fist back

to chamber position as fast as or faster than you shot it out.

From a solid fighting stance, push off your rear foot and extend your rear-elbow while you snap your arm out like a whip, striking with the knuckles on the back of your hand (figs. 7–9).

Hook Punch

The hook punch is most common to boxers, kickboxers, and full contact fighters. The hook punch is best used at close range because one can best utilize the power of the body during the weight transfer. That is, when you shift your weight from you rear foot to your front foot as you turn your hips into the punch. Do not swing at your target wildly. You must keep the

elbow bent at approximately 90-degrees in order to maintain proper form. It is also important to strike with the two knuckles closest to the thumb. In street confrontations it is fairly common when someone throws a hook punch that they break their hand on the target because they strike with the weakest two knuckles furthest away from the thumb. The reason why these two knuckles are the weakest is because they are aligned with the forearm.

From a solid fighting stance, push off your rear foot and step forward with your front foot. Turn your hips forward while keeping your rear-elbow bent on 90-degree angle and strike your target (figs. 10–12).

Ridgehand Strike

The ridgehand strike is generally used to strike soft tissue areas like the throat, eyes, groin, mid-section, nose, and sometimes the temples. If not executed correctly by striking exactly with the side of the knuckle closest to the thumb, it is easy to seriously damage the hand. What sometimes happens is instead of hitting the target with the side of the knuckle, the practitioner hits with the fingers, dislocating them or even breaking them.

The ridgehand strike is generally used as a defensive measure against a charging opponent, as the defender slips off to the side and hangs him with it. In a situation where an opponent has you in a side-headlock you could perform an upward ridgehand strike to the groin to soften him up to loosen his grip.

From a solid fighting stance, push off your rear-foot and step forward with the lead foot. Turn your hips forward while keeping your rear-elbow on a 45-degree angle and strike your target (figs. 13–15).

Horizontal Knifehand Strike

The horizontal (palm down) knifehand strike is geared more for the street because it is designed for striking soft tissue areas. Striking the throat is one of the most popular and effective maneuvers for incapacitating an opponent quickly with this technique. Striking to the base of the skull is another good area to hit using the knifehand.

To execute the horizontal (palm down) knife hand, begin in a solid fighting stance, push off your rear-foot as the lead-foot steps forward. Extend your elbow and snap your arm into the target using the knife-edge of the hand (figs. 16–18).

The horizontal (palm up) knifehand strike is useful to strike the temple and neck. It can also be used to immobilize your opponent's arms. I do not recommend this technique as an opening attacking technique because in order to get any real power out of the technique you must draw your hand close to your ear,

which is very telegraphic. I would recommend this technique in more of a defensive situation, say after a block or deflection type technique.

To execute the horizontal (palm up) knife hand, begin in a solid fighting stance, bring your rear-hand up to the side of your head, push off your rear-foot, and step forward with your front-foot. Turn your hips forward and strike your target with the knife-edge of the hand (figs. 19–21).

Spearhand Strike

The spearhand strike is most effectively used against soft tissue areas like the throat. Even though some people practice the strike to the mid-section, it is highly dangerous and should be avoided in a real confrontation, as it is very easy to break your fingers on such a hard surface. It takes years of specialized training and conditioning to do a proper spearhand, which very few martial artists practice.

From a solid fighting stance, push off of your rear-foot and step forward with your lead-foot. Extend your lead-elbow and strike the target with your extended fingers (figs. 22–24).

Palm Heel Strike

The palm heel strike is probably one of the most powerful hand techniques in all of martial arts because of its simplicity and stability. Just about anyone can learn this technique and you don't have to have strong wrists because the heel of the palm (the striking area) is perfectly aligned with the forearm. Some of the best areas to strike using this technique are the nose, eyes, mouth, temples, and the back of the head.

From a solid fighting stance, push off your rear foot and step forward with your lead foot. Turn your hips forward and extend your rear hand, striking with the palm-heel portion of the hand (figs. 25–27).

Undercut Punch

The under-cut punch is most useful at close range and targeted at the mid-section, ribs, kidneys, and groin. I have found that this technique can be easily executed even while being right up against your opponent. It has a tendency to look a little scrappy, but what the heck—even if you don't score with the judges it may open your opponent up for a technique that will. When properly executed, an opponent can easily be winded or dropped, especially in a bare-knuckle fight.

From a solid fighting stance, push off your rear foot and step forward with your lead foot. Extend your rear elbow (while keeping the palm facing up), striking the target with the two knuckles closest to the thumb (figs. 28, 29).

Uppercut Punch

The uppercut punch is typically seen in boxing, kickboxing, and other full contact martial arts. This punch is best executed at close quarters in order to generate the most power from the body. The best time to execute the uppercut to the head is when the opponent's upper body or head is leaning forward so you can make clean contact. The best time to execute the uppercut to the body is when you're almost right up against your opponent.

Many don't understand the difference between the uppercut punch and the undercut punch because they can sometimes look the same when executed, depending on the situation. The difference between the two is that the undercut is delivered in a straight line, like a jab, except usually much lower and the uppercut scoops upward in the same manner in which you would use a shovel and can be used to the head, body, and groin.

From a solid fighting stance, push off of your rear foot and step forward outward on a 45-degree angle (opening up the hips for power and ease of motion). Pivot your hips and keep your elbow bent approximately 90-degrees and drive the fist upward, striking the target with the two knuckles closest to the thumb (figs. 30–32).

Rear Elbow Strike

The rear elbow strike is best executed at close range and is designed for power. To get the most power out of this strike you must synchronize the whip of your elbow with the turning of your upper body into the target. If they are done separately you will lose power.

From a solid fighting stance, push off of your rear foot and step forward with your front foot while turning your upper body forward (keeping your forearm parallel to the floor), striking the target with your elbow (figs. 33–35).

Lead Elbow Strike

The lead elbow strike is best executed at close range and generates
its power from the simultaneous
whip of the elbow and turning
of the upper body. Generally
this technique lands easiest to
the head.

From a solid fighting stance,
push off your rear foot and

step forward with your
front foot while turning
your upper body forward
(keeping your forearm
parallel to the floor),
striking the target with
your elbow (figs. 36–38).

Upward Elbow Strike

The upward elbow strike is best executed from close range and aimed at the mid-section or head. Elbow strikes make exceptional finishing blows and can be practiced in combinations using target pads or a punching bag.

From a solid fighting stance, push off your rear foot and step forward with your front foot while turning your upper body forward and striking upward with your elbow to the target area (figs. 39–42).

Jabbing Elbow Strike

The jabbing elbow strike is a close range technique generally used in street self-defense situations. Most of its power comes from the snapping of the shoulder, which propels the elbow into the target.

From a solid fighting stance, push off your rear foot and step forward with your front foot, striking the target area with your lead-elbow (figs. 43–45).

Chapter 7
STANDING KICKS

Rear Leg Kicks

Rear Leg Front Kick

From a solid fighting stance, raise your rear-knee to aim toward your target, extend your knee, and snap your kick into your target with the ball of the foot or the heel (figs. 1–3).

Rear Leg Roundhouse Kick

From a solid fighting stance, raise your rear knee, pivot on the ball of the lead foot, and snap your foot into the target using the instep or ball of the foot (figs. 4–7).

Rear Leg Axe Kick

From a solid fighting stance, bring your rear knee up to your chest, extend your foot up high above your shoulders or head, and bring your foot down hard on the target, striking with the heel or flat of the foot (figs. 8–11).

Rear Leg Inside/Outside Crescent Kick

From a solid fighting stance, bring your rear knee to your chest on a 45-degree angle (to the inside of your body) and extend your foot while swinging your knee to the outside of your body, striking with the instep (figs. 12–15).

Rear Leg Outside/Inside Crescent Kick

From a solid fighting stance, raise your rear knee to your chest on a 45-degree angle to the outside of your body and extend your foot while swinging your knee to the inside of your body, striking with the heel or the arch of the foot (figs. 16–19).

Rear Leg Sidekick

From a solid fighting stance, raise your rear knee up to chamber position, pivot on the ball of the foot of the lead leg, and snap the lead foot into the target using the heel or blade of the foot (figs. 20–23).

Lead Leg Kicks

Lead Leg Front Kick

From a solid fighting stance, slide your rear foot up to your lead foot, raise your lead knee to chamber position, and snap your leg into your target with the ball of the foot or the heel (figs. 24–27).

Lead Leg Roundhouse Kick

From a solid fighting stance, slide your rear foot up to your front foot (toes pointing in the opposite direction of the kick), raise your knee to chamber-position, snap your foot into the target using the instep or ball of the foot (figs. 28–31).

Lead Leg Sidekick

From a solid fighting stance, cross your rear foot behind your lead leg (pointing your heel in the direction of the kick), raise your knee to chamber position, and snap your foot into the target striking with the heel or blade (figs. 32–35).

Lead Leg Hook Kick

From a solid fighting stance, cross your rear foot behind your lead leg (pointing your heel at the intended target), raise your knee to chamber position, extend your heel out on an angle slightly away from the target, and sweep your foot across the target, striking with the heel or the flat of the foot (figs. 36–41).

39

40

41

Lead Leg Axe Kick

From a solid fighting stance, bring your rear foot up to your lead foot, raise your lead knee to your chest, extend your foot up high above your shoulders or head, and bring your foot down hard on the target, striking with the heel or flat of the foot (figs. 42–46).

Lead Leg Outside/Inside Crescent Kick

From a solid fighting stance, slide your rear foot up to your front foot, raise your front knee to your chest on a 45-degree angle (to the outside of your body). Extend your foot while swinging your knee to the inside of your body, striking with the heel or the arch of the foot (figs. 47–51).

Spinning Kicks

Turn Back Kick

From a solid fighting stance, turn your buttocks toward your target while looking over your rear shoulder at the intended target. Raise your rear knee to chamber position and extend your leg out straight, striking the target with your heel (figs. 52–55).

Spinning Roundhouse Kick

From a solid fighting stance, spin toward your blind side, stepping forward with your rear foot, switch sides (turning your back to your opponent for a split-second), raise your rear knee to chamber position, then snap your foot into the target using the instep or ball of the foot (figs. 56–62).

Spinning Crescent Kick

From a solid fighting stance, turn your back to your target, raise your rear-knee to your chest, and spin on your lead foot, striking the target with the instep (figs. 63–66).

Chapter 8
JUMPING KICKS

I do not believe that learning jump kicks is necessary for the martial artist to be a master fighter. In fact, most jump kicks usually don't land properly and can leave the practitioner in a rather awkward position.

However, I also believe that (if you do not suffer back or joint problems) jumping kicks can be used as a powerful training tool. For example, jumping up high can increase power and strength in the calves and thighs. Being able to hit a target accurately with a jump kick develops muscle coordination, balance, timing, and a realistic perception of three-dimensional space. Another benefit of jump kicks is that they can be a lot of fun for the martial artist because they can add a little spice to your workout.

Pop Kicks

A pop kick is a jump kick, which does not cover much distance, and is usually done for close-range fighting or counter-attacking.

Jump Front Kick

From a solid fighting stance, bend your knees, jump straight up into the air, raise your rear knee up high, and execute a front kick, striking with the ball of the foot (figs. 1–4).

Jump Roundhouse Kick

From a solid fighting stance, bend your knees, jump straight up into the air. While turning your hips counter-clockwise chamber your right knee and execute a back leg roundhouse kick, striking with the instep or ball of the foot (figs. 5–8).

Jump Sidekick

From a solid fighting stance, bend your knees and jump straight up into the air. While simultaneously chambering your leg for the kick, execute a sidekick, striking with the heel (figs. 9–12).

Flying Kicks

A flying kick is a jump kick that is usually used for attacking from a medium or far-range.

Jump Front Kick

From a solid fighting stance, swing your rear knee up high, propelling your body up off the ground and execute a front kick while in mid-air. The higher you swing your knee up and the faster you do this the higher your jump will be (figs. 13–16).

Jump Roundhouse Kick

From a solid fighting stance, swing your rear knee up high, propelling your body up off the ground, and execute a roundhouse kick, striking with your instep or ball of the foot. Make sure you roll your hips over in mid-air while executing this kick (figs. 17–20).

Jump Sidekick

From a solid fighting stance, step forward with your front foot and then push off with your front foot to propel yourself through the air. With your body sideways, and your rear leg in chamber position, execute a sidekick

striking with your heel. Make sure your buttocks are facing your target as you kick for maximum power (figs. 21–25).

Jump Turn Back Kick

From a solid fighting stance, step forward while switching sides and bend your knees slightly like coiled springs, jump straight up into the air, and execute a turn-back kick, striking with your heel (figs. 26–30).

Step-Through Turn Back Kick

From a solid fighting stance, lift your rear knee up and pivot clockwise, switch sides in mid-air, chamber your knee like a sidekick, and execute a turn-back kick, striking with your heel (figs. 31–35).

Jump Axe Kick

From a solid fighting stance, swing your rear knee up high, propelling your body upward, extend your front foot high above your head, and drop the axe kick downward, striking with your heel or the flat of your foot (figs. 36–40).

Jump Hook Kick

From a solid fighting stance, bend your knees, jump straight up into the air and chamber your knee like a sidekick and execute a lead leg hook-kick (figs. 41–44).

Jump Spinning Hook Kick

From a solid fighting stance, bend your knees, jump straight up into the air while pivoting counter-clockwise, chamber your rear foot like a sidekick, and execute a spinning hook kick, striking with the flat of your foot or the heel (figs. 45–48).

Jump Spinning Crescent Kick

From a solid fighting stance, step forward with your rear foot switching sides, bend your knees, jump straight up into the air, pivot counter-clockwise, and execute a spinning crescent kick, striking with the side of the heel or the instep (figs. 49–54).

Part Three

TRAINING

Chapter 9
ATTRIBUTE TRAINING

Strength is measured by the amount of force one can exert through movement. Muscular strength is required in all phases of fighting, thus the development of strength is essential.

Power is measured by how fast a given mass covers a given distance. Although mass and speed are the two main components of power, in fighting there is another factor that constitutes power.

That factor is proper form. Proper form enhances one's ability to utilize their legs, arms, hips, and weight in unison to maximize power.

Balance is how weight is distributed during any movement or technique. Good balance is essential in all forms of combat, including ground wrestling.

Let's now examine exercises to train these attributes.

Balance and Strength Exercises

Front Lunge

From the standing posi-
tion, step forward with
your left foot into a long
stance with your front
knee bent at a 90-degree
angle while your rear foot
is up on the ball and your
rear knee is bent. Repeat
10 or more times per leg
to strengthen the thighs
and hamstrings (figs. 1, 2).

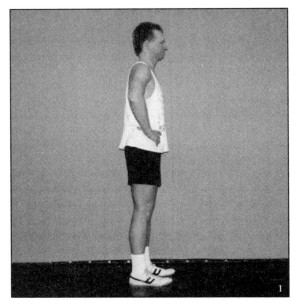

Squat-Kick Drill

From a standing position with your guards up and your feet one shoulder-width apart, squat until your thighs are parallel to the floor and stand up straight and then execute a front snap kick to the head or mid-section. Repeat 10 or more times per leg to strengthen the thighs (figs. 3–6).

Step Lunge

Start with your right knee bent, right foot flat on the floor, and your left leg straight with heel on the floor and toes pointing up. Push off of your right foot as you shift over to the opposite side, trying to move as smoothly as possible throughout. Repeat 10 or more times per side to strengthen the thighs and hamstrings (figs. 7–9).

Individuals who have serious knee injuries may wish to avoid this exercise due to the stress that is exerted on the joint.

Side Leg Raise

While lying on the floor, roll onto your left side with your left hand supporting your head and raise your right leg as high as possible without feeling discomfort. Do 10 or more per side per workout to strengthen the obliques, abdominals, and back muscles (figs. 10, 11).

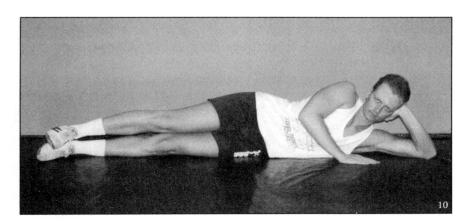

Inverted Leg Straddle

While lying flat on your back with your feet straight up in the air, open your legs until you reach the point of tension and then slowly return to the starting position. Do 10 or more repetitions per workout to strengthen the inner thighs (figs. 12, 13).

As a variation, ankle-weights can be added for more intensity for advanced practitioners. However, don't overdo this exercise in the beginning because it is very easy to pull a muscle in your legs. As it takes some time before you can really get intense with this exercise, work up the repetitions slowly.

Leg Raise

While lying on the floor, place your hands underneath your buttocks for support and raise

your heels six inches off the floor (with thighs touching each other) and then slowly raise your legs up off the floor until they are pointing at the ceiling. Do 10 or more per workout to develop the lower-abdominals (figs. 14, 15).

To add intensity, keep your head a couple inches off the floor and/or add ankle weights. If you have neck or back problems you may wish to keep your head flat on the floor to avoid pain and possibly pulling a muscle.

Alternate Leg Extensions

While lying on your back, place your hands underneath your buttocks and pull your knees inward and alternately extend them in and out. Do 10 or more repetitions per side per workout to strengthen the lower abdominals (figs. 16, 17).

For more intensity raise your head a few inches off the floor, keep your heels lower to the floor, and/or add ankle weights. If you have neck or back problems you may wish to keep your head flat on the floor to avoid pain or a pulled muscle.

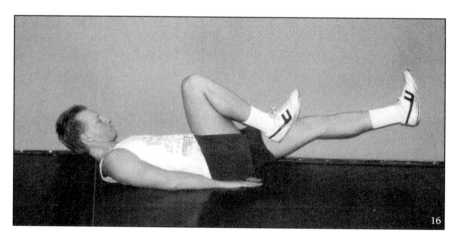

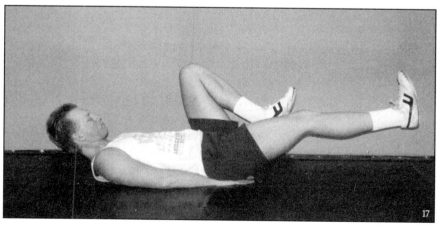

Ab Crunches

Utilizing an abdominal isolator device, place your hands on top of the padded area, with your knees bent, and your head on the head rest gently curl up (by tensing your stomach muscles) lifting only your upper body up off of the ground. Do 20 or more repetitions per workout to strengthen the upper-abdominals (figs. 18, 19).

This is probably the safest available method for abdominal development for those who suffer from neck and back problems.

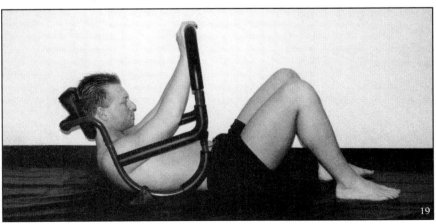

Chair Training

Chair training is used to develop good balance in kicking. Through the use of a chair one can get used to the proper position of the legs, hips, and upper-body without fear of falling-down. To gain a certain skill one must sometimes use training wheels to accomplish a given task. In this case the chair is considered the training wheels which in time can be removed.

Sidekick Extensions

Using a chair for balance, chamber your knee in side-kick position and then extend your foot out and hold for two to five seconds. Do 10 or more extensions per leg per workout to strengthen the buttocks and legs (figs. 20, 21).

Sidekick Leg Raise

Using a chair for balance, point your toes towards the chair and look over your left shoulder, then raise your left leg up using the strength of your buttocks only until you reach your range of mobility. Do 10 or more raises per leg per workout (figs. 22–25).

Control, Balance, Proper Form #1

From a solid fighting stance, raise your right knee to chamber position and slowly extend out a front kick without touching the chair, retract your leg back to chamber position, and then step back down to a solid fighting stance. Do five or more per leg per workout to strengthen the legs, develop leg control, improve balance, and learn proper-form (properly chambering the knee for front kicks) (figs. 26–29).

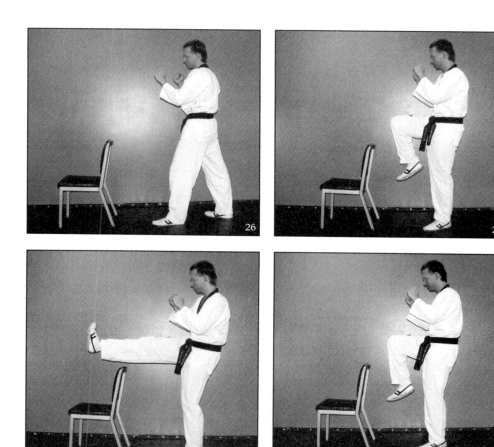

Control, Balance, Proper Form #2

From a solid fighting stance, slide your rear foot up chambering the lead leg in a sidekick position, and slowly extend your leg out without touching the chair, retract your leg back to chamber position, and then return to a solid fighting stance. Do five or more per leg per workout to strengthen the legs, develop leg control, improve balance, and learn proper-form (figs. 30–33).

Leg Extensions

While lying flat on your back, place your hands underneath your buttocks, pull your knees inward toward your chest and extend your legs outward. Do 20 or more per workout to strengthen the lower abdominals. On extension, the closer your heels are to the floor the more intense the exercise becomes (figs. 34, 35).

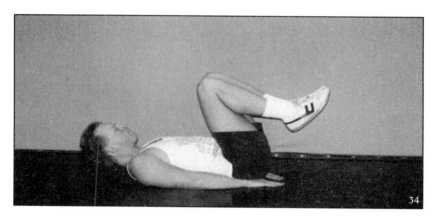

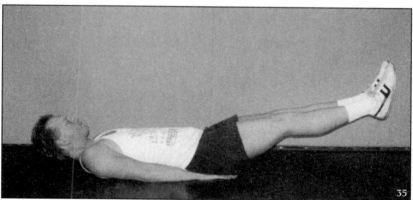

Chair Push-Ups

With your hands either flat or in knuckle position on two chairs, and your feet up on a bench or other chair, gently lower yourself down until your chest is lower than the seat of the chair, then push straight up, returning to the starting position. Do 20 to 30 repetitions to strengthen the chest and triceps (figs. 36–38).

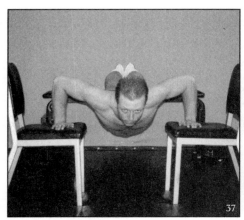

Wheel-Barrow

Have a partner grab hold of your ankles while you walk on the palms of your hands. Try to average a distance of 20 or more feet per set to strengthen the chest and triceps. Be sure to gently lower your partner's legs to the floor when they are finished to avoid smashing your partner's knees (fig. 39).

Calf-Raises

While in the standing position place the balls of your feet on the ledge of any solid surface which is two or three inches higher than the ground and go up unto your tip-toes by contracting your calf muscles. Do 20 to 30 per set to strengthen the calves (figs. 40, 41).

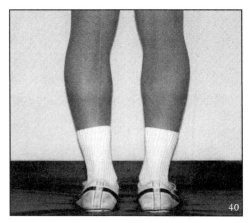 

Single Leg Hop

From the standing position grab hold of your left foot with both hands, hold it in front of you, and hop forward covering distance without losing your balance. Try to cover 20 or more feet per leg to strengthen the calves and develop good balance (fig. 42).

Control Drills

Low and High Roundhouse Kick

From a solid fighting stance, slide your rear foot up to your front foot and execute a lead leg roundhouse kick to a low target, retract your leg back to chamber position and execute a roundhouse kick to the higher target (figs. 43–46).

Hook and Roundhouse Kick

From a solid fighting stance, slide your rear foot up to your front foot and execute a lead leg hook kick to one of the targets from the inside of the two targets, then execute a lead leg roundhouse kick to the target across from it without dropping your foot (figs. 47–49).

Forward Hop and Kick

Utilizing a partner with a target hop on one foot and execute lead leg roundhouse kicks as you travel across the room (figs. 50–52).

Front and Side Kicks

From a solid forward fighting stance execute a front kick, retract your leg to chamber position without dropping your foot, and then execute a sidekick directly behind you (figs. 53–55).

360-Degree Pivot Kicking

Without dropping your foot to the floor execute a lead leg roundhouse kick to the front of you and retract your leg to chamber position. Without dropping your foot to the floor pivot 90-degrees on your supporting foot and execute a roundhouse kick, retract your leg to chamber position. Repeat until returning to a solid fighting stance facing in the same direction as you started. When finished you should have pivoted a full 360-degrees. Do five or ten circle (repetitions) per leg to strengthen the legs and develop balance and muscle control (figs. 56–59).

Advanced practitioners may wish to perform two to three complete 360-degree pivots before dropping their foot to the floor for more of a challenge. This drill can also be done with other kicks like front kick, sidekick, and hook kick.

58

57

156

Chapter 10
SPEED TRAINING

Speed is the amount of time required to cover a given distance. Speed is one of the greatest assets a fighter can have. Unfortunately even to this date very few martial artists have been given the knowledge and skills required to develop speed on a mental and physical level.

Avoid Telegraphing

Telegraphing your intentions to your opponent has two effects on your speed. The first one is that your moves take too long to execute and the second is that your opponent has more time to prepare to counter your attack.

The following photographs illustrate the difference between a telegraphic and non-telegraphic technique.

Kicking (Telegraphic)

Some people when executing a rear leg roundhouse kick lean way back on their supporting leg, thinking that they will be able to develop more power in their kick from the momentum of the weight transfer. However, since your pre-movement alerts your opponent to your attack you can be countered or evaded easily. There are better ways to generate more power than swinging like a caveman (figs. 1–3).

The proper way to start any kick is from a balanced fighting stance, revealing nothing to your opponent. You want to make a straight line or direct path to your target.

Kicking (Non-Telegraphic)

The following photos illustrate the correct starting point for kicking. Your foot should only go in a straight line forward (figs. 4–6).

Punching (Telegraphic)

The most common mistake people make when punching is pulling their fist back and then punching. By doing this you are warning your opponent to your intent and are slowing down your move-

ment. If you pull your fist back your weapon is going in the opposite direction first and this is illogical and dangerous for combat purposes (fig. 7).

Punching (Non-Telegraphic)

To be non-telegraphic when punching you must punch in a straight line from the chamber-position (or the on-guard position) to the target. Once again you must go in a straight line from point A to point B (figs. 8, 9).

Speed Relaxation Drills

Speed relaxation drills are designed to train your muscles to stay loose until the moment of impact in order to develop more speed in your techniques. The working muscles can move faster if all the muscles not in use for the technique also remain relaxed. Remember that these drills are designed for relaxation and not for power, so don't snap your foot out as hard as you can.

Front Punch

From a fighting position relax all the muscles in your body including the muscles in your face, especially the neck, shoulders, arms, and hands. Shoot out a front punch as fast as possible while remaining relaxed and without losing proper form. Perform this 10 times per arm in the air and then another 10 times per arm using a striking target (figs. 10–12).

Reverse Punch

From a fighting position relax all the muscles in your body, including the muscles in your face, especially the neck, shoulders, arms, and hands. Shoot out a front punch as fast as possible while remaining relaxed and without

losing proper form. Perform this 10 times per arm in the air and then another 10 times per arm using a striking target (fig. 13).

Lead Leg Roundhouse Kick

From a relaxed fighting stance slide your rear foot up to your front foot, relax your body as much as possible, then snap out a lead leg roundhouse kick. Return back to your original starting place. Perform this 10 times per leg in the air and then another 10 times per arm using a target (figs. 14–17).

Speed Acceleration Drills

Kick, Drop, Kick

Utilizing the lead leg stand in front of a target that is approximately at your belt level and kick the target as fast as you can 10 to 20 times, trying to make each kick faster than the last (by building up momentum). Switch sides and kick with the other leg. Remember to relax all muscles not involved in the exercise. Also emphasize the relaxation of all muscle groups around the hip area before impact (fig. 18).

Speed-Jab Drill

Utilizing the lead arm stand in front of a target that is approximately your head level and jab punch the target as fast as you can 10 to 20 times, trying to make each punch faster than the last by building up momen-
tum. Remember to keep your whole upper-body as relaxed as possible before impact (fig. 19).

Speed Vertical Punch

From a forward stance, execute vertical punches at mid-section or head-level as fast as you can, trying to make each punch faster than the last by building up momentum. Each punch should come over top of the previous, sort of like pedaling a bike with your hands. This drill can also be done with a target or air shield (figs. 20–23).

Speed Combination Drills

The purpose of speed combination drills is to teach the mind and the body to flow without hesitation from one movement into the next. They will also program the combinations into your muscle memory, thus reducing the amount of thinking or lag time before spontaneous execution in a real situation.

Drill #1

From a solid fighting stance execute a lead vertical punch, then a rear vertical punch, then another lead vertical punch to your opponent's face, followed by a lead leg roundhouse kick to his mid-section. Execute this combination five to 10 times per side per workout (figs. 24–28).

Once you have memorized this combination try to increase your speed every time you practice. Also try timing your combination with a stop watch every couple weeks to check your improvement.

Drill #2

From a solid fighting stance step forward on a 45-degree angle to the opponent's blindside on the outside of his lead foot. Deflect his lead hand, knocking it down with your open lead hand, trap his wrist/forearm area with your rear hand (palm-down), and then execute a backfist strike to his head. Execute this combination 10 times per side per workout (figs. 29–32).

When you practice make sure you bring your backfist back to chamber position as quickly as you snapped it out, just in case you need to hit your opponent again. This is so that in a real situation you'll be ready.

Drill #3

From a solid fighting stance, step forward with your front foot and deflect your opponent's lead guard downward with your lead open hand. Trap your opponent's lead hand with your rear hand, execute a lead vertical punch to his head, followed by a rear vertical punch to his head, and finish with another lead vertical punch to his head. Execute this combination five to 10 times per side per workout (figs. 33–38).

Drill #4

From a solid fighting stance
step forward with your front
foot and deflect your opponent's
lead guard with a lead open hand.
Trap your opponent's lead guard
with your rear open hand (palm-
down), slide your rear foot up to
your front foot, execute a lead leg
axe kick to the opponent's head,

followed by a lead leg roundhouse kick to his mid-
section, followed by another lead leg roundhouse kick to his
mid-section, and finishing with a lead leg roundhouse kick to
his head. Execute this combination five to 10 times per side
per workout, with a rest of five to 10 seconds so that you can
deliver each movement with full speed (figs. 39–49).

Reaction Time Drills

Reaction time drills are designed to lower the time it takes you to react or retaliate to a given stimulus, like a punch to your head. There are three different types of reaction time drills: 1) audio-cueing, 2) visual-cueing, and 3) realistic visual-cueing.

Audio-Cueing Drill

An audio cue is a sound that signals you to do something. In taekwondo training the most common audio cue is the *ki hap* or yell.

Stand in a fighting stance facing a target. As your opponent yells, execute a lead leg roundhouse kick as fast as you can to the target. Do this 10 times per leg per session.

Note that this exercise can be done using any punch or kick. Make sure your partner yells with different lengths of pause in between so you do not preempt the cue. Remember, this is a reaction drill.

Visual-Cueing Drill

Visual-cueing is when you react to some sort of visual stimuli, like a hand signal.

Stand in a fighting stance facing a target. As your opponent opens his closed fist (for example), execute a lead leg round-house kick as fast as you can to the target. Do this 10 times per leg per session.

Note that this exercise can be done using any punch or kick. Make sure your partner opens his fist with different lengths of pause in between so you do not preempt the cue. Remember, this is a reaction drill.

Realistic Visual-Cueing

A realistic visual-cue is a cue that is familiar to the environment in which you are training. In taekwondo, an opponent charging after you with a punch or kick is a realistic visual-cue. The following are some examples of this:

Sidekick vs. Jab

As the opponent attacks with a jab punch lean back and execute a lead leg sidekick to the rib-cage. Perform this five to 10 times per side (fig. 50).

Hook Kick vs. Reverse Punch

As the opponent attacks with a reverse punch lean back and execute a lead leg hook kick to the head. Perform this five to 10 times per side (fig. 51).

Lead leg Roundhouse Kick vs. Jab

As the opponent attacks with a jab punch lean back and execute a lead leg roundhouse kick to the head. Perform this five to 10 times per side (fig. 52).

Punch Combination vs. Knifehand Strikes As your opponent
attacks with a jab punch execute an open lead hand block to
the inside of his left wrist. As your opponent attacks with a
reverse punch execute a rear hand palm block to the outside
of the right wrist. Execute a knifehand strike with your right
hand to the opponent's rib-cage, a knifehand strike with your
left hand to the opponent's face, a knifehand strike with your
right hand to the opponent's rib-cage again, and then finish
with a knifehand strike to the opponent's face with your left
hand. Perform this combination 10 times per side per workout
(figs. 53–59).

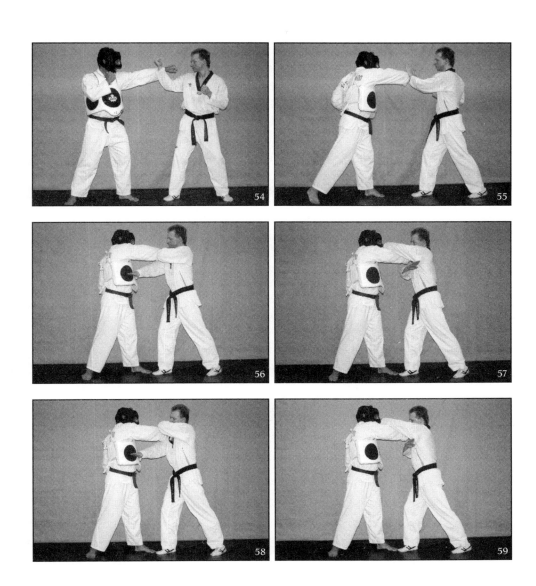

Punch Combination vs. Blocking/Vertical Punches As the opponent attacks with a jab punch execute a lead outside palm block to the outside of his left wrist. As the opponent attacks with a reverse punch execute a rear hand outside palm block to the outside of his right wrist. Execute a lead vertical punch to his head, a rear vertical punch to his head, a lead vertical punch to his head, and finish with a rear vertical punch to his head. Perform this combination 10 times per side per workout (figs. 60–66).

Distance in Relation to Speed

The following examples of countering the opponent by varying your stance will give you an idea of how you can intercept (or hit) your opponent faster by understanding the principles of distance.

Incorrect Distance

The attacker attempts to strike with a back leg kick to the mid-section and the defender tries to counter with a defensive side-kick by just leaning his weight back onto the supporting leg while in a fairly wide side stance. The end result is the opponents either smash shins or the attacker winds up kicking the defender's knee (figs. 67, 68).

The reason this doesn't work is because the distance between the defender's supporting leg (while kicking) is too far away from the attacker to allow the kicking leg to intercept the opponent before the back leg roundhouse kick finishes it's trajectory. Therefore, the attacker and defender simultaneously jam each other's technique. This is a very common incident in sparring which most people overlook, including black-belts.

Lead Leg Side Kick vs. Rear Front Kick

The defender starts off in a regular side stance. The defender decides he wishes to intercept any incoming attack from his opponent with a defensive sidekick, so he pulls his rear foot up to his front foot with only a few inches separation between. As the opponent attacks the defender lets go of a powerful side-kick to the mid-section while the attacker is still on one foot unable to complete his kick (figs. 69, 70).

The technique worked this time because the defender pulled his supporting leg closer to the target. Therefore, the defender had to cover less distance to strike his target than in the first example. Thus, we've provided a way to make our counter-attack more time-efficient by making the distance shorter. The shorter the distance the shorter the time it takes to reach your target. Also, by making your supporting foot closer to the opponent you have increased your reach by many inches.

Lead Leg Front Kick vs. Rear Front Kick

From the same position as in Fig. 69 (with your feet approximately six inches apart), as soon as you see your opponent move forward execute a lead leg front kick to the mid-section. Repeat five to 10 times per leg (fig. 71).

Turn Back Kick vs. Back Leg Roundhouse Kick

From the same position as in Fig. 69 (with your feet approximately six inches apart), as soon as you see your opponent move forward execute a turn-back kick to the mid-section. Repeat five to 10 times per leg (fig. 72).

Back Leg Roundhouse Kick vs. Back Leg Roundhouse Kick

From the same position as in Fig. 69 (with your feet approximately six inches apart), as soon as you see your opponent move forward execute a back-leg roundhouse kick to the mid-section. Repeat five to 10 times per leg (fig. 73).

Back Leg Front Kick vs. Rear Roundhouse Kick

From the same position as in Fig. 69 (with your feet approximately six inches apart), as soon as you see your opponent move forward execute a back leg front kick to the mid-section. Repeat five to 10 times per leg (fig. 74).

Spinning Hook Kick vs. Rear Roundhouse Kick

From the same position as in Fig. 69 (with your feet approximately six inches apart), as soon as you see your opponent move forward execute a spinning hook-kick to the head. Repeat five to 10 times per leg (fig. 75).

Lead Punch vs. Rear Roundhouse Kick

As your opponent executes a back leg roundhouse kick step forward with your front foot and execute a lead hand vertical punch to your opponent's mid-section. Repeat five to 10 times per leg (figs. 76, 77).

Chapter 11
BREATHING AND RECUPERATION

Proper Breathing

Proper breathing is necessary in combat and competition because the body's demand for oxygen is extremely high as the muscles are working much harder than usual.

When you don't breath properly the brain and the muscles won't get their required amount of oxygen and therefore won't function correctly. If those demands are not met the following symptoms will arise: fatigue, sluggishness, poor muscle control, inability to think logically, poor timing, lack of power, lack of speed, poor endurance, hyper-ventilating, possibility of vomiting, and possibility of passing-out. The last two may seem a little extreme, but they do happen occasionally.

Breathing (with & without a mouth-guard)

When training or fighting without a mouth guard the proper way to breath is to inhale through your nose and exhale through your mouth.

When training or fighting with a mouth guard a typical breathing pattern is to take a long breath in through your nose and two short breaths out from your mouth. You may wish to design your own breathing pattern if you do not like this one.

Endurance Training

In order to have excellent breathing patterns for combat one must practice their breathing patterns during sparring and during all intense endurance exercises and drills.

Kicking and Striking

When kicking or striking always exhale as you snap your arm or leg out, as this gives you more power.

Recuperation Tips

When enduring the rigorous training as a serious martial artist you will suffer from stiffness, sprains, strains, bruises, cuts, scrapes, and possibly even broken bones—all requiring a recuperation process to heal. With regards to preventative measures, not much can be done about the last three other than keeping strict rules for sparring and training. But for the others there are some very efficient methods available. The following are some tips for recovering from your workouts and injuries at a faster rate than normal.

Warm-ups and Stretches are required before all workouts to prevent injuries that are caused by cold (stiff) muscles and joints.

Cool-down Stretching is required after all work-outs to prevent muscle cramps and soreness due to your muscles, ligaments, and tendons shrinking back to regular size too fast and lactic acid building up. If you stretch after your training session you will increase your circulation, flushing some of the lactic acid out of your muscles and slowing down the stiffening-up process.

Inversion Exercises, such as standing on your head against a wall for about five minutes, will increase your circulation and flush lactic acid out of the muscles. This is highly recommended to do right after you are finished your workout.

Water Therapy is commonly used by professional athletes who endure anywhere from between four to eight hours a day of training/exercise. Hot and cold water are used to once again increase blood circulation to prevent stiffness.

Contrasting Shower Therapy is when you take a hot shower for about three minutes (washing your body and your hair as usual) followed by a cold shower for about 30 seconds to a minute.

When you take the cold shower start by placing your arms and legs into the cold water first and then the center of your body and then your head. Never take a cold shower first and then the hot one because you will ruin the effect.

Sauna/Jacuzzi Therapy is when you go into a hot sauna or jacuzzi until it gets too hot for you and then you immediately take a cold shower. By heating up the muscles, ligaments, cartilage, and other soft tissues, it makes them more elastic and flexible which in turn makes them more efficient for exercise and combat. Keep in mind that sauna and jacuzzi therapy should always be done after your workout and not before, as heat has a tendency of making athletes sleepy.

Always take a warm or hot shower first before you go into a sauna to help clean out the pores in your skin. Otherwise if you take a cold shower after your sauna the cold water will make your pores close up, immediately trapping any dirt or sweat inside them causing little dots or sometimes pimples to appear all over your body.

Ample Sleep and Rest is a very important factor in recuperation because your body prefers to do most of its repairing while you are sleeping. Most serious athletes require anywhere from between eight to 12 hours of sleep a day to stay healthy and injury free from their demanding workouts.

Chapter 12
DIET AND NUTRITION

Excellent nutrition is one of the key elements for successful training and fighting. To make nutrition a little easier to understand, I offer brief examples of its importance.

When it comes to cars and jet planes inferior fuel will not produce efficient energy production for the vehicle's motor or engines to perform properly. Also, if one continues to use inferior fuel or the wrong kind for that specific type of vehicle, they will eventually ruin the engine.

The human body works in much the same way. If you put inferior fuel (junk food) into your system your body will not perform to its maximum potential while training or fighting. The type of food you eat affects your endurance, strength, coordination, and your overall mood. Processes of the brain required for fighting, such as concentration, reaction-time, and decision making skills, are greatly affected by nutrition as well. The following are recommended foods and vitamin supplements for the serious martial artist:

Vegetables that are deep orange or dark green are the best to eat because they contain the most amount of nutrition (energy). The best orange vegetables to eat are squash, yams, sweet potatos, and carrots. The best green vegetables to eat are broccoli, spinach, kale, and asparagus.

Fruits are an excellent source of quick energy, especially the ones that are mostly composed of liquid, like oranges and grapefruits. Bananas are probably the most nutritious, but require much more time to digest and should not be eaten five minutes before a workout. And if you feel you need a quick energy pick-me-up before working out or competing, it is best to drink any type of 100% pure fruit juice about 10 to 15 minutes beforehand.

Meat is probably one of the most difficult topics to come to a conclusion, as some say it causes cancer, heart-attacks, high-cholesterol, and other ailments in the human body and should thus be avoided. Others say that you need meat in your diet to maintain sufficient amounts of protein and you may get sick if you don't get it.

Probably the best answer to this problem is to only eat meat that has the lowest fat content, like poultry and fish, and avoid eating any area of the animal which contains high amounts of fat. Another solution is to replace meat with food that is high in protein and has only natural fats found in vegetation. This replacement is composed of beans (e.g., tofu, kidney beans, black beans, lentils, etc.) and seeds/nuts (e.g., peanuts, almonds, coconuts, sunflower seeds, etc.).

Grains are extremely important for producing the high amounts of energy needed for training and fighting. Brown rice, pasta, whole wheat breads, and oats are some of the most typically consumed by fighters to enhance their energy levels.

Dairy Products are closely related to meat products and should not be eaten too heavily. If you like to drink milk, drink 1% milk as it contains less fat.

Vitamin Supplements recommended for heavy martial arts training include vitamin-A, B-complex, vitamin-C, ginseng, ginko biloba, the essential amino-acids, and vitamin-E.

Juicing is a popular method of getting more vitamins out of food without having to eat more of it. The body can much more quickly process and utilize liquids than solids. Juicing is typically done with fruits and vegetables and has been popular for decades.

Part Four

SPARRING STRATEGIES

Chapter 13
OFFENSIVE STRATEGIES AND COMBINATIONS

Direct Attack

A direct attack is when a fighter does not utilize any deceptive tactics (e.g., faking, feinting, or footwork) before executing a kick, punch, or strike.

Indirect Attack

An indirect attack is when a fighter utilizes deception to set-up his opponent for a kick, punch, or strike. Deception can be in many forms such as faking, feinting, combination attacks, broken rhythm attacks, footwork, and programming of the opponent.

Faking

A fake is a movement that creates a reaction in your opponent's defensive composure, which allows you to dictate what your next move will be. By faking and causing a reaction in your opponent you can create openings that would not normally exist without this strategy. A fake must cover distance and can utilize footwork, punching, striking, and/or kicking to obtain a reaction in your opponent. Keep in mind that faking can be one of the most powerful methods of scoring on your opponent safely and is also a powerful method of giving you early clues as to what your opponent's strategy will be during the rest of the fight.

Feinting

A feint is any head and/or body movement used to throw an opponent's timing and defensive skills off in order to set-up a kick, punch, strike, or combination attack. This tactic is very typical in combat sports like boxing and can be very useful in other combative sports.

Combination Attack

A combination attack may be two or more techniques thrown in a row. Usually a combination attack's purpose is to use the preceding techniques as a set-up for the last technique thrown–which is meant to do the damage. This is not a solid rule, though. A fighter may land all techniques thrown in a combination or almost all of them, depending on the situation at hand.

Broken Rhythm Attack

A broken rhythm attack is when a fighter uses a change in direction, or a change in speed, in order to set-up his opponent to score.

Programming

Programming is when you do something over and over again to your opponent to create a false reality for them to become comfortable with. This false sense of reality triggers the fighter into reacting the same way every time, giving you a mental advantage. This advantage is that he is expecting something that you will change when he least expects it, allowing you to score.

Attacking Methods

Combination Attack

From a solid fighting stance, slide your rear-foot up to your front foot, execute a lead leg sidekick to the opponent's hip to draw his guards down low, retract your foot, and execute a lead leg roundhouse kick to the head.

Combination Attack

From a solid fighting stance, slide your rear foot up to your front foot, execute a lead leg sidekick to the opponent's hip, drawing his guards down low, retract your foot, and execute a lead leg roundhouse kick to his head.

Combination Attack

From a solid fighting stance, slide your rear foot up to your front foot, execute a lead leg roundhouse kick to the opponent's mid-section, drawing his guards down low, drop your foot down to the floor and execute a lead leg hook kick to his head.

Combination Attack

From a solid fighting stance, slide your rear foot up to your front foot, execute a lead leg roundhouse kick to your opponent's head, enticing him to lean his head out of range to avoid the kick. Retract your foot to chamber position and then execute another lead leg roundhouse kick to his head.

Combination Attack

From a solid fighting stance, slide your rear foot up to your front foot, execute a lead leg roundhouse kick to your opponent's head, enticing him to lean his head out of range to avoid the kick. Drop your foot to the floor and execute a lead leg roundhouse kick to his mid-section.

Combination Attack

From a solid fighting stance, slide your rear foot up to your front foot to execute a lead leg roundhouse kick to the opponent's mid-section, drawing the opponent's guards down low. Retract your foot to chamber position, and execute a lead leg roundhouse kick to the opponent's head.

Combination Attack

From a solid fighting stance, slide your rear foot up to your front foot, execute a lead leg roundhouse kick to the opponent's mid-section, then drop your foot to the floor. Execute another lead leg roundhouse kick to the mid-section to draw the opponent's guard down, retract your foot, and execute a lead leg roundhouse kick to his head.

Combination Attack

From a solid fighting stance, slide your rear foot up to your front foot, execute a lead leg roundhouse kick to the opponent's head, causing him to lean his head out of range. Drop your foot to the ground and execute a lead leg hook kick to his head.

Combination Attack

From a solid fighting stance, slide your rear foot up to your front foot, execute a lead leg roundhouse kick low to the mid-section to draw the opponent's guards down, retract your foot, execute a hook kick to his head.

Probe Kick Set-Up

From a solid fighting stance, execute a probing roundhouse kick to your opponent's head, causing him to lean his head out of range, and return as fast as possible to your original starting point. Execute another probing roundhouse kick to your opponent's head (programming him to believe that he only has to lean his head slightly out of range to avoid being hit) and return as fast as possible to your original starting point. Step forward with your front foot as fast and deep as possible, quickly slide your rear foot up to your front foot and execute a lead leg roundhouse kick to his head, this time scoring.

Probe Kick Set-Up

From a solid fighting stance, execute a probing roundhouse kick high toward the opponent's head, causing him to lean his head out of range. Return as fast as possible back to your original starting point. Execute another probing roundhouse kick toward his head, programming the opponent to think he only has to lean his head out of range to avoid being hit. Again return as fast as possible to your original starting point and execute a very deep gliding sidekick the his mid-section, this time scoring.

Probe Kick Set-Up

From a solid fighting stance, execute a probing roundhouse kick toward the opponent's head, causing him to lean his head out of range. Return as fast as possible back to your original starting point. Execute another probing roundhouse kick toward his head, programming the opponent to think he only has to lean his head out of range to avoid being hit. Return as fast as possible back to your original starting position and execute a deep gliding roundhouse kick to the face, this time scoring.

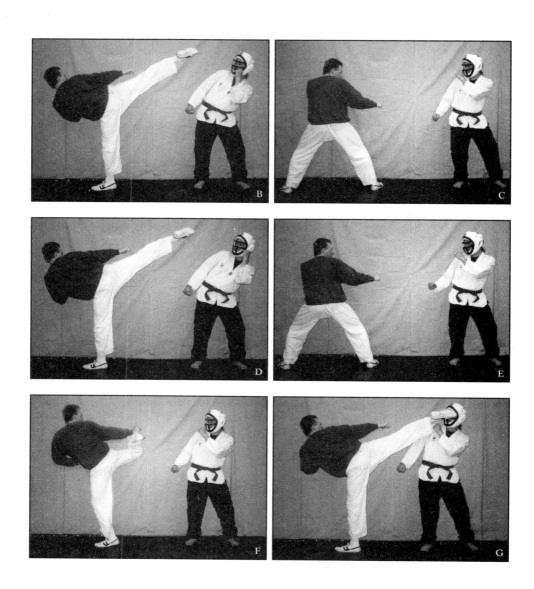

Probe Kick Set-Up

From a solid fighting stance, execute a probing roundhouse kick
toward the opponent's head, causing him to lean his head out
of range. Return as fast as possible back to your original starting
point. Execute another lead leg roundhouse kick high toward
the opponent's head, programming him to think he only has to
lean his head out of range to avoid being hit and that it is safe
to counter. Drop your foot to the floor, and as the opponent
attempts to execute a counter back leg roundhouse kick (as he
thinks it's safe to retaliate), immediately execute a turn back
kick to his mid-section.

Probe Kick Set-Up

From a solid fighting stance, execute a quick lead leg round-house kick high to the head, causing the opponent to lean his head out of range. Drop your foot down to the floor, causing your opponent to think that he can score on you at a moment of weakness (in this case, regaining your balance after kicking). As your opponent attempts to execute a counter back leg round-house kick, intercept his attack with a stopping sidekick to the mid-section.

Combination Attack

From a solid fighting
stance, execute a lead
leg sidekick, causing
your opponent to
take a step back to
get his body out of
range. Drop your foot
to the floor to cause
your opponent to
think that he can
score on you at a

moment of weakness (in this case-regaining your balance after
kicking). And as your opponent attempts to execute a counter
back-leg roundhouse kick, intercept his attack with a lead leg
roundhouse kick to the head.

Combination Attack

From a solid fighting stance, execute a lead leg roundhouse kick toward the opponent's head, causing him to lean his head out of range. Drop your foot to the floor, causing your opponent to think that he can score on you at a moment of weakness (in this case, regaining your balance after kicking). As the opponent attempts to counter with a lead backfist, lean back (moving your head out of range), and execute a hook kick to the head.

Combination Attack

From a solid fighting stance, slide your rear foot up to your front foot and execute a backfist toward your opponent's head to draw his guards up high to protect his head and leave his mid-section exposed. Execute a lead leg roundhouse kick to the mid-section.

Combination Attack

From a solid fighting stance, execute a lead leg roundhouse kick low to the opponent's mid-section to draw his guards down, step down in front, and execute a backfist to his head.

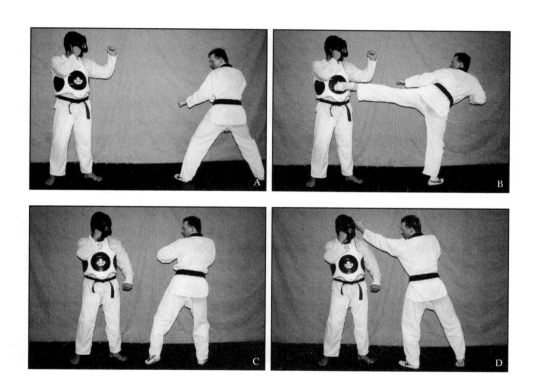

Combination Attack

From a solid fighting stance, slide your rear foot up to your front foot and execute a backfist high toward the opponent's head, drawing his guard up high, and execute a sidekick to his midsection.

Combination Attack

From a solid fighting stance, step forward with your front foot and quickly execute a jab/reverse punch combination toward the opponent's head to draw his guards up high. Lean back out of range of the opponent's counter back-

fist strike, and then execute a lead leg roundhouse kick to his mid-section.

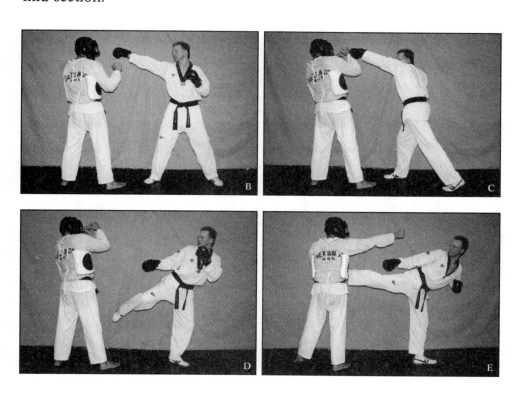

Combination Attack

From a solid fighting stance, execute a lead leg roundhouse kick high toward the opponent's head, drawing his guard up high, step down in front, and execute a backfist strike on the opposite side of his head.

Combination Attack

From a solid fighting stance, step forward with your front foot and execute a jab punch to the opponent's mid-section to draw his guard down. Slide your rear foot up to your front foot as your opponent blocks your punch.

Lean back out of range as your opponent retaliates with a counter reverse punch, and execute a lead leg hook kick to his head.

Combination Attack

From a solid fighting stance, step forward with your front foot and execute a jab punch to the opponent's mid-section, enticing him to block and lower his guard. Lean back out of range of your opponent's counter reverse

punch and execute a lead leg roundhouse kick to his head.

Combination Attack

From a solid fighting stance, step forward with your lead foot, execute a jab punch with your lead hand to draw the opponent's guards up to expose his rib-cage. Execute a turn back kick to the opponent's rib-cage or midsection.

Combination Attack

From a solid fighting stance, execute a roundhouse kick to the opponent's mid-section to draw his guards down low. Drop your foot down directly in front of your opponent. Execute another roundhouse kick to the opponent's mid-section to program him to think that your goal is to score on that area so he will be pre-occupied with protecting it. Drop your foot down directly in front of your opponent again, and then execute an extremely fast lead leg hook kick to his head.

Probe Kick Set-Up

Starting from a solid fighting stance, execute a probing sidekick close to the opponent's mid-section and return to your original starting point as fast as possible. Execute a probing lead leg roundhouse kick at the opponent's head, enticing him to block the left side of his head. Return back to your original starting point as fast as possible, and execute an extremely fast hook kick to the right side of the opponent's head.

Probe Kick Set-Up

From a solid fighting stance, step forward with your front foot and execute a jab punch at the opponent's head to draw his guard up and expose his ribcage or mid-section. From here you can execute a lead leg roundhouse kick to his mid-section, or execute a sidekick to his knee.

Scramble Step Attack

From a solid fighting stance, step to your right off the line of attack with your right foot, and then execute a push step back to your left, again moving off the line of attack. Now that the opponent's line of focus is disturbed, execute a lead leg round-house kick to his mid-section.

Circular Footwork Attack

From a solid fighting stance, step to your right with your left foot, pivoting slightly on your right foot. Step with your right foot to the right again and trail your left foot with you. (At this point you should have made a quarter of a circular turn with your footwork around the opponent). Now change directions and push step off your front (right) foot to your left, step with your left foot, and execute a lead leg roundhouse kick before your opponent can regain his balance.

Circular Footwork Attack

From a solid fighting stance, step to your left with your left foot and bring your right foot up to your left foot. Step to the left with your left foot. At this point you should have made a quarter circle around your opponent. Trail your right foot to wind up almost in front of your left,  while still moving to your left, and change directions by stepping with your left foot to your right. Draw your right (or lead foot) in toward your rear foot, step forward with your front foot, then execute a sidekick to your opponent's head.

Offensive Open-Side Cut footwork

From a solid fighting stance, step with your rear foot to your open side to entice your opponent to shift his position. Pull your front foot to your rear foot, step forward with your front foot, quickly slide your rear foot up to your front foot, and execute a lead leg roundhouse kick.

Indirect Attack

From a solid fighting stance, step your rear foot 45-degrees to your blindside to entice your opponent to shift his position. Quickly pull your front foot to your rear foot, and then step forward with your front foot

toward your opponent. Execute a back leg roundhouse kick to his mid-section or head.

Indirect Attack

From a solid fighting stance, step your rear foot to your open side to entice your opponent to shift his position. Pull your front foot up to your rear foot, then again step with your rear foot to your open side to again entice your opponent to follow you. Draw your front foot to your rear foot, step forward with your front foot, slide your rear foot up to your front foot, and execute a lead leg roundhouse kick to the mid-section or head.

Indirect Attack

From a solid fighting stance, step your rear foot 45-degrees to your blind side to entice your opponent to shift his position. Draw your front foot up to your rear foot again and step your rear foot 45-degrees to your blind side to again entice your opponent to shift his position. Draw your front foot up to your rear foot, step forward with your front foot, and execute a back leg roundhouse kick to the opponent's mid-section or head.

Indirect Attack

From a solid fighting stance, step your front foot up to your right and weave your upper body to the right to get your opponent's attention. Push off your front foot to your left to again get your opponent's attention, and quickly slide your rear foot up to your front foot and execute a lead leg axe kick to the head.

Broken Rhythm

From a solid fighting stance, step your rear foot to your open side to draw your opponent's attention. Replace your rear foot with your front foot and immediately step back to your original spot with your rear foot. Pull your front foot to your rear foot, quickly slide your rear foot up to your front foot, and execute a sidekick to the mid-section.

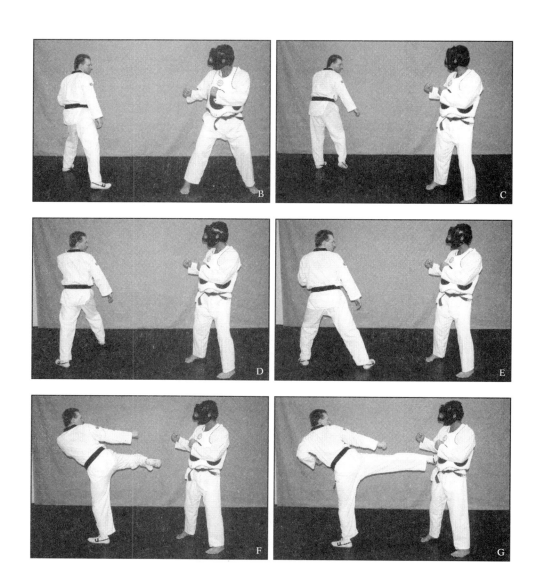

Blind-Side to Open-Side Fake

From a solid fighting stance, with your rear foot step backward on a 45-degree angle to your blind side, bring your front foot to your rear foot to entice your opponent to follow you disturbing his line of focus. With your rear foot step across to your open side to again entice your opponent to follow you. Step forward toward your opponent with your front foot, and execute a cross behind sidekick to his mid-section.

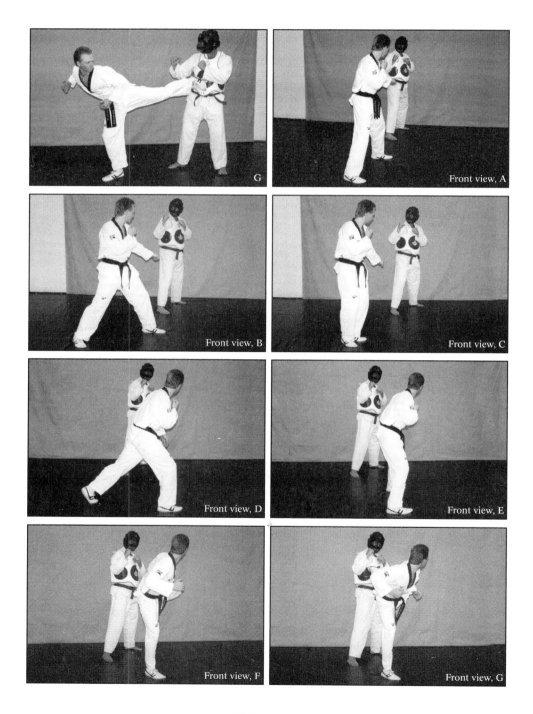

G

Front view, A

Front view, B

Front view, C

Front view, D

Front view, E

Front view, F

Front view, G

Broken Rhythm

From a solid fighting stance step backwards with your rear foot about 8-12 inches. Trail-in your front foot an equal amount of distance, slide your rear foot to your front foot as you see your opponent step forward to even up the distance. Step forward with your front foot and execute a spinning hook-kick to the opponent's head.

Chapter 14
DEFENSIVE STRATEGIES AND COMBINATIONS

There are many different defensive strategies or methods a fighter can execute in order to defend himself. When I speak of methods, I refer to actual fighting concepts that can be applied in any system of martial art. To understand only one concept/method of defense will limit your ability to adapt to the limitless situations that can arise in competition or in the street. Depending on the fighter's mental and physical abilities certain methods will become more natural than the others to execute. To say that one method of defense is superior to another is not logical because the history of martial arts has proven to us that anybody can be beaten— they just have to meet the right opponent that will make their defense crumble.

Direct Counter Attack

A direct counter attack is when a fighter kicks or strikes an opponent defensively as they attack. A direct counter attack is done without the utilization of footwork, blocking, jamming, or any other preparatory method of maneuvering used to open their opponent up for an attack. In other words, it is kicking or striking as soon as you see your opponent move, utilizing the correct technique that will protect you while striking your opponent before he can finish his attack.

The direct counter attack requires high concentration, precise timing, and great speed to be effective. Most beginners do not have this skill naturally and usually have a hard time developing it without hours of dedicated training.

In my opinion it is the most difficult and advanced method of counter-attacking, but is the most effective because of the physics involved, as your opponent's momentum is moving forward toward you just as yours is moving toward him. Like two trucks in a head-on collision, the damage can be tremendous.

Advantages

- Maximum power of your counter-technique is utilized.

- It is hard to be set-up by a combination fighter.

- Constant practice of these types of counter attacks will develop sharp reaction time.

- Increased concentration and ability to seize opportunities to attack.

- Physical speed usually increases because the fighter is forced into concentrating on moving fast as he has to hit his target before his opponent finishes his technique.

- Hitting your opponent before they can finish their technique consistently throughout the fight will cause him to be frustrated and lose confidence in his abilities. Frustration also causes a fighter to expend more energy than is required, as mental stress drains you physically.

Disadvantages

- If you are slow or not properly trained your counter will either be jammed or you will get hit.

- It requires split second timing and not a moment of hesitation or indecisiveness.

- As you must be fully committed to your technique, and have very little chance to disengage or change tactics in the middle of execution, if an unforeseen problem arises you may be hit.

Indirect Counter Attack

An indirect counter attack is when a fighter utilizes preliminary movement (preparatory measures) in order to execute the counter kick or strike.

Advantages

- Allows the fighter more time to establish what technique will be used to counter attack.

- Easier to disengage because you are not fully committed to your counter attack.

- If you sidestep using footwork after or before your opponent throws or finishes his first technique, you can avoid getting set-up by a combination fighter.

- Indirect counter-attack drills will enhance your ability to quickly create or find openings in an opponent.

Disadvantages

- You can be easy prey to combination fighters if you block or back-up in a straight line before you counter kick or strike.

- If you're backing up and then countering, your power may be lost.

- If your opponent is much larger than you, your technique may bounce off them if you are moving backward.

Countering Against the Dancer

If you spend any amount of time in the ring you will come across many different types of fighters who utilize different kinds of approaches. One of those fighters is the "dancer." The dancer will utilize deceptive footwork in order to attack his opponent without fear of being countered on their approach. The dancer usually uses circular and side-to-side footwork in an effort to keep their opponents off balance.

The following are some tips that will help you to defeat the dancer:
- Use body and head feinting and faking techniques first (without committing yourself to an attack) to disturb the opponent's rhythm and force them to stay stationary long enough for you to attack safely.

- Utilize lateral footwork to cut-off the opponent or corner him.

- Only allow engagement with the opponent from close range as the dancer is typically a long range fighter.

When facing a dancer it is best to disengage from him entirely and head to the opposite side of the ring (keeping your eyes on him the whole time of course), thus reversing the game as now he has to chase after you if he wants to hit you. It's the theory behind the old "playing cat and mouse" concept. The dancer is usually considered as the mouse and the more stationary opponent who tries to chase after the dancer is the cat. By taking off to the other side of the ring you entice that annoying mouse to temporarily change his routine. He has to come to you now if he wants to score, which in turn can put you in a good position to score because you have just turned him into the cat, slowing him down. You could call it a fish out of water example. Taking an opponent out of his environment is one of the most powerful combat strategies in existence.

Jamming

Jamming is when a fighter short-circuits his opponent's movements or smothers the opponent's arms and legs using his own limbs. The strategy of jamming is excellent when facing someone who is a weak close range fighter, someone who has a reach advantage over you, or on those who depend highly on combination attacks.

Body-Pivot Evasion with Forearm Deflection

From a relaxed standing position an opponent is facing you with a knife pointed at you. As he steps forward to thrust it into your mid-section pivot your body sideways deflecting the knife with your forearm (away from your body).

Body-Lean Evasion

From a solid fighting stance, as the opponent attacks with a kick to your head lean your head out of range.

Body-Lean Evasion

From a relaxed standing position, as the opponent attacks with a straight punch, weave to your left and then counter with a right ridge hand strike to his head.

Body-Lean Evasion

From a relaxed standing position, as the opponent attacks with a straight punch, bend at the hips to weaving to your right and execute a palm heel strike to the opponent's mid-section.

Front Foot Draw

From a solid fighting stance, draw your front foot to the rear foot, sidestep left with your front foot, draw your rear foot up to your front foot, and execute a hook kick to the opponent's head.

Weaving Evasion

From a relaxed standing position (square to your opponent), as your partner attacks with a straight punch bend at the hips to weave out of range. Keep your knees slightly bent.

TAEKWONDO'S PHILOSOPHY

Philosophy for Training

When training in the martial arts one must always have a goal or destination in mind to be successful. In order to gauge how hard to train, how many days a week to train, and what techniques to focus on, you must first have an established goal in mind, no matter how far-fetched it may sound to your friends, family, or fellow martial artists. In most cases you should have a time frame in order to properly gauge a reasonable strategy of how you're going to accomplish this goal.

When the time comes when you have accomplished your goal don't just be content with that. Instead, concentrate on how you could have done even better than you did so the next time you do something similar it will become a higher quality victory.

If you did not accomplish your goal do not think of it as a failure, rather think of what you've done as an experiment and/or a learning experience in which you have to keep adjusting the variables until you reach the right combination for victory. Also, you must be very honest with yourself when doing an evaluation after you succeeded or failed to attain your goal.

If you failed to reach your goal, match up all the requirements necessary with what you actually did when making your attempt and don't make excuses or lie to yourself to make it all right, or you will never know what really went wrong. Did you come up short of the requirements needed to accomplish your goal? Did you miss some of your workouts or get lazy and only workout for an hour when you were supposed to workout for six hours?

The funny thing is that the people who live their lives like this are the people who usually never achieve their goals because they constantly make false fronts for themselves when they get lazy.

Philosophy for Competition

To be successful in competition you need to want to win because if you're there just to survive you may not be aggressive enough to take advantage of situations in which you can score on or knockout your opponent. Never concern yourself with losing, only think about how you are going to win.

In order to control your fear you must totally understand what it is you are afraid of. Many people are afraid of losing and looking stupid. Nobody likes to look bad, but anyone who's been in martial arts for any reasonable length of time will have a bad day and find themselves on their butt in front of a crowd of people, so just deal with it when it happens.

I myself have no problem with this type of fear because as far as I'm concerned this is just part of everyday life. If somebody puts you down, just stand back up, brush off the dirt and continue like nothing has happened. You always have another chance at redemption as long as you're still alive.

A lot of people are afraid of the pain involved while fighting so they avoid, whenever possible, sparring and tournaments. My personal fear is not pain (I can deal with pain), but of being seriously injured and not being able to practice martial arts any longer. This is probably the only fear that a serious martial artist has because pain and moments of embarrassment are just a part of learning and an unavoidable part of martial arts. Someone who's life's passion is martial arts is taking a big risk every time they walk into the ring because if something seriously goes wrong they could lose what they have worked so hard for, for many years, and this can add quite a bit of pressure to the situation.

The best thing that one can do is make sure that they are properly prepared for an upcoming event to avoid any possible accidents and this will relieve some the pressure knowing you are capable of keeping things under control.

Philosophy for Combat

The right mental attitude to have for real combat (self-defense and fighting) is quite a bit different than for competition. In competition it is not the real thing. If you give up, the fight will be stopped by the referee. In real combat you can lose your life if you give up. In real combat there are no rules so a concept like poor sportsmanship because a fighter cheated does not exist.

Basically in real combat you must be prepared mentally to fight to the death using whatever means necessary to win regardless of the moral implications set by society. In a competition you do not have to make that type of commitment, which is why tournaments are more suited for a less disciplined individuals than street fighting.

It is a common story to hear of black belts, masters, and tournament champions being badly beaten and even killed by less skilled opponent's because they were not mentally prepared to deal with a life threatening situation. They had the tools, the offensive strategies, the defensive strategies, and the physique to handle their opponent easily. So what happened to these guys? Was it a fluke? Does martial arts not really work in real combat?

Probably the closest answer to the truth is that they just froze because when training in the gym it is always a controlled environment and this information is stored in the same place as all your combative knowledge with a direct connection. That direct connection is what makes people freeze up and hesitate because having someone come at you for real puts you in an unfamiliar setting, causing your brain to take extra time processing new variables and spitting out unneeded garbage which is not required to get the job done.

When someone picks a fight with you the most common first reaction is to try to understand what you did to make this guy want to kill you. On the average if you had no foreknowledge of this person popping up out of nowhere, and fighting was not on your mind, you will probably just stand their in shock and become nervous. Your brain says, "What should I do? Should I hit him? Will I make this worse if I attempt to do anything? Should I try to talk to them? Should I just run? Am I going to get my head kicked in? Will I be dead in few seconds?"

This is the kind of garbage that floods through your brain inside of split seconds, blocking off the channels that are connected to your martial arts training and combat attitude which you needed the moment the altercation started.

The question is how does one create that link without going out to the bars looking for a fight or brawl to participate in?

The answer is mental training. Whenever you practice your moves in class don't just go through the movements. Pretend it's the real thing. Visualize every intimidating aspect of a real encounter, by tapping directly into your emotions.

If you are sitting around doing nothing, visualize in your head dealing with your worst nightmare and winning.

Also on a regular basis you must convince yourself that you have the perfect right to defend yourself even if that means seriously injuring your opponent, and thus you will not hesitate, you will only act.

Philosophy for Life

The life lessons that can be learned through martial arts training are endless. Many people think that martial arts are just about fighting and there is nothing more to them. After being in martial arts for many years I've come to discover that they are a very intense study of man. They are ways of looking deep inside ourselves and others to discover hidden strengths and weaknesses. Although on the outside it may all seem very physical, it really isn't. Your body is only a tool which expresses your mind and spirit.

If you want something large in life you must go after it with all of your heart or you probably won't get it. And if you get it too easily you will fail to appreciate it and have very little respect for others who have accomplished the same or are trying to.

In conclusion, I would like to say that my martial arts training has given me the strength and power to overcome obstacles that most fear to face and that in writing this book my hope is to pass that strength onward to others.

"Remember to believe in yourself always, because all is possible if you never give up!"